To Linda —
Sister & friend I love
so dearly —

Carl

Giving Away Simone

Giving Away Simone

A Memoir

Jan L. Waldron

RANDOM HOUSE

The names and identifying characteristics of some family members, friends, and doctors in this book have been changed to protect their privacy. All pseudonyms are marked with an asterisk at first mention in the text.

Copyright © 1995 by Jan L. Waldron

Library of Congress Cataloging-in-Publication Data

Waldron, Jan L.
    Giving away Simone : a memoir / by Jan L. Waldron. — 1st ed.
        p.   cm.
    ISBN 0-8129-2400-2
    1. Waldron, Jan L. 2. Birthmothers—United States—Biography.
    3. Adoption—United States—Psychological aspects. I. Title.
    HV874.82.W35A3 1995
    362.82′98′092—dc20
    [B]   94-30132
                                                                          CIP

Book design by Susan Hood
Manufactured in the United States of America
9 8 7 6 5 4 3 2
First Edition

*To the memory of my grandmother Altie H. Smith,
and for Carlos, Pepe, and Rebecca*

Acknowledgments

First and most important I would like to thank Daughter Rebecca for her loving support of this book.

I owe many thanks to Merrill Black, my reader, so often my memory, my critic, and my friend without whose wicked wit, brilliance, and warmth I cannot imagine life itself.

I want to thank my brother, GHW, for the care, loving challenges, and encouragement he has offered in my life, and to this book. And many thanks are owed Laura Perkins for her thoughtful reading of the first draft, for her part in this story, and for so much more.

I will always appreciate Eleanor Majewski for her invaluable friendship and her rare understanding of the issues of adoption. When I felt alone in my often uncommon views, her clear-sighted opinions and support provided, from the start, much needed company.

I would like to thank Sue Hertz for making the idea of writing a book seem within reach, and for encouraging me to use the first-person singular; and I would like to thank the Women of Wednesday Night for the midweek refuge they have provided for the past fourteen years.

I want to thank Lisa Horwitz, a friend, for her help in finding articles, books, thoughts relevant to adoption, and for sharing her experience as an adoptee.

For his faith and auspicious advice, I am especially grateful to my agent, David Black; and for his insight and suggestions, I am thankful to Lev Fruchter.

I want to thank Betsy Rapoport, my editor, for her enthusiasm, guidance, and intelligence throughout.

I will always be grateful to my sons for their generous understanding of this story. Because they have shown me so many times how deep a parent's love can be, they have helped me understand what Rebecca's parents have given her.

I cannot imagine writing this book without the harbor of a loving partner. For me, this person has been and continues to be David McPhail, who listened to every word of this story first with patience and a precise ear and who never veered from absolute belief in this book, and in me. For his place in my life and in the lives of my children, I owe the deepest gratitude of all.

Sylvia Spears★

|

Clara Jones,★ 1872–1964

|

Mavis Peabody★ (birthmother), b. 1908
Altie Hayes Smith (adoptive mother), 1901–1984

|

Ruth Ann Murphy,★ b. 1934
(renamed Sara Eugena Smith★)

|

Jan Waldron (birthmother), b. 1951
Linette Farrell★ (adoptive mother)

|

Simone Waldron, b. 1969
(renamed Rebecca Anne Farrell★)

Contents

A u t h o r ' s   N o t e

Silence, fables, and lies have created, by omission, our culture's idea of adoption. In the past, when we thought about adoption, we saw floral-bordered frames of fatefully joined families; we segued, smiling, to pictures of languishing babies being scooped up into the wanting arms of solvent Christian couples—a benevolent match of destinies. But the unspoken irony of adoption is that one family's luck is another's loss and the relinquished child is as much a part of the family that is losing her as she is a member of the family that grows.

Now, with stories of biological relatives reclaiming their children months, sometimes years, after they have legally relinquished them, natural parents are being perceived in a new and unsettling light—as confused retrievers of unwitting kids caught in a cruel tug-of-war. It is unfortunate (and suspect) that most of the long-due attention given birthparents, finally deemed newsworthy, has been so troubling.

As long as we believe and embrace partial pictures, adoption will teeter between two extremes: It will hold its benevolent place in our culture, up there with charitable causes and the work of God, or it will reside tenuously on the edge of an underworld, threatened by plotting birthparents who want to grab back the babies they *thought* they wanted to give away.

When will we stop selling the movie?

★ ★ ★

I hated the idea of adoption when I was young. It had, I knew, hurt my mother (adopted when she was sixteen months old), and when I was eleven my mother had left us, recoiling slowly but inevitably into the wombed comfort of her orphanhood. She couldn't make her own motherhood last. Later, she would say she had created herself "without birth-determined allegiances, based on a party of one." Worst of all, I had contracted the tendency myself, and at seventeen had given away a baby of my own.

Why couldn't our family keep our children? Why did we keep losing our mothers? My blood-related great-great-grandmother, great-grandmother, grandmother, and mother had all turned away from their children. Fifth in line, I fought an undertow of conditioned exiting, an affliction of easy farewells.

After eleven years of sitting on the secret of her existence, I met again the daughter I had given away. In the fifteen years since, Rebecca and I have worked hard at what's referred to, in adoption language, as "reintegration," which means we are always trying to get used to each other and to figure out just what kind of relatives we are.

We have been inquisitors, we have searched and destroyed—each other and ourselves—for the answers that would make sense of a life's worth of missing, weaving in between our necessary truces until the next rueful outpouring, brittle silence, or giddy afternoon. And we love each other beyond speech—against a backdrop of doubt, across an unbridgeable distance. How do I answer the looming question she lives with: Why? and the doubt that nags me. What do I owe her, how do I give it?

For the birthmother, the adoptee, the adoptive parents, and their families, the acts of surrendering and adopting a child cut to the heart of what kinship means: What makes a mother? When is a child a daughter? An honest, open-minded view of the issues inherent in adoption can provide insight to anyone who lives within, or at a troubled distance from, a family of his or her own.

This story is about family values. More closely, it is about Rebecca and me, maddeningly original, in search of our own personal kinship. It is about the overlapping, intersecting families in our lives, the mothers before and the children after. It is a story of mothers and daughters, and the wounds and aggressive expectations imposed by our moody intimacy and chronic symbiosis interruptus; and, as women, our slow dancing, cheek to smoothly similar cheek, breast to breast, hip to congruous hip in sacred and infuriating alikeness.

There is no agency in the federal government that collects data on adoption. So the work of fact collecting and dispersal has been left to the dangerously biased National Committee on Adoption. The committee has compiled a book called *The Adoption Factbook* (NCA, 1989), which includes "facts" such as "When unwanted pregnancy occurs, adoption ought to be an option considered more often." The three-page chapter titled "Birthparent Issues" includes information about "how well birthmothers do after they decide to place the baby for adoption." You can just hear the baby-cute bounce in the committee's oft-repeated preference for "the adoption option."

Because the number gathering is chiefly authorized by proadoption (antichoice) groups, the stories of the people behind the statistics subscribe to a well-worn format. After the baby is delivered and then adopted, the birthmother has done her deed and is expected to retire gratefully from the picture. Hopefully she succumbs to the implicit request for her absence and rarely attempts to alter her image, much less to exist. Only when we probe socially convenient images, and refuse, as birthrelations, merely to survive as muted numbers, undercover, can we begin to understand honestly the experience of adoption.

There are approximately 6 million adoptees in the United States. By extension, there are 12 million birthparents and 12 million adoptive parents—30 million people directly involved in adoption. Add to that number the untraceable millions of other birth and adoptive relations, and the percentage of our population touched by the act of adoption grows beyond imagination.

In the nineties, there will be record numbers of birthrelations looking for each other. The babies born during the peak years of U.S. adoptions—1969 and 1970—have reached their young twenties, and they are searching now.

I no longer hate the idea of adoption. It gave me a grandmother I will never forget and brought my daughter to parents who love her. And I know the possibility of adoption can help heal the losses suffered by women and men incapable of having children they so desperately crave. There is hardly a day I do not feel inordinately lucky that I have been able to have children of my own; I do not presume and have never presumed the bounty of their existence. The loss of my first child (through adoption) left me, at least, with the promise of my ability to make another; that promise took me through the worst of my grief, and I cannot begin to know what it must be like to live without that hope. What I want to say in this book in no way diminishes the hope adoption can offer to childless families.

But I am tired of the willful romanticizing and reactionary rhetoric the experience seems to spawn. The legal appropriation of a child is hardly an isolated act, free from history and emotional aftermath. The word we use, *adoption,* describes merely one part of a complicated experience. Our collective rejection of the other parts and people—which include birthrelations, surrender, and often search and reunion— blacks out significant phases of the same experience. In this country we are having a terrible time confronting the whole story, in all its sorrow, joy, and turmoil.

This book is about one woman's experience. I have not attempted to proclaim a universal truth, because in matters of adoption there are none. Moreover, I would not presume such a position. But I do write with an urgency, to get the word out, to flaunt this honest story in an area in which sedated platitudes have presided far too long. There are stakes, beyond the personal, in the telling of this story.

The upside of the current confessional climate in this country, in which women who sin and tell populate television talk shows, is the undoing of a conspiracy to erase ourselves and the effort to give life to the stories we've been expected to hide. (There are millions of birthmothers in this country, yet most people will tell you they've never met *one.* Nearly as many will tell you they don't know what a birthmother is.)

There is still an almost Victorian pathos about a birthmother's secretive history; she is guilty of sins so extreme even she begins to question her blackened soul. When she gives away her baby, she is not just altering her and her child's future, she is snubbing bedrock institutions: Motherhood and Family. She is insubordinate.

When we, the bad girls, agree to keep quiet, we support the conforming social view that our experiences (sexuality, unplanned pregnancy, rejected motherhood, our losses) are negligible. And often when women finally begin to speak, inching out of our isolations, we are caught in yet another compromise; the source of our candor, we justify, erupts from our involuntary experiences and not from our voluntary voices. We defer to the experience as the protagonist, removing ourselves still. When we take full responsibility for our place in the story, we can speak boldly, on our terms; we dare our censors to see us.

The arrogant presumption of our Supreme Court to determine a woman's procreative rights, the current flurry of oversimplified adoption "theories," and the media-infused dramas concerning postadoption custody have fueled the writing of this book as much as my own story has shaped it. But my immediate response is to the so-called right-to-life movement, which sells adoption as an adorable idea to vulnerable girls and women who cannot know the whole truth.

For antichoice activists, the life of a child is never more valuable than when it resides within a woman. Federally funded assistance for student mothers and working parents, and the right of born children to be fed and educated, is never part of the plan of proadoption protesters. In the womb, the infant is the pitiable innocent product of unrestrained sex. The newborn must then be separated promptly, at the time of its full-term birth, from its stained cradle, its punishable maker. For some birthright believers, the first flogging for the sexually free girl is the hasty removal of her baby.

There is a great deal of ambiguity native to adoption, so many manufactured scenes mined with doubt and wishful thinking, preserved by simple ignorance because so much has been left unsaid. The fallout of this choice is far more tangled than we are led to believe or are willing to know. The costs are high.

Women are trained to sacrifice many things for the greater good. But we cannot agree to give over our babies, selflessly, quietly, painlessly; it is not in our nature. In the end, it is essential for real images to emerge in the adoption picture. Not to recall sorrow, or to demand pity, and certainly not to blame; but to remind us all that giving away a baby is a profoundly unnatural act from which there is never full re-covery.

As the mother of a baby I gave away, the parent of two children I have kept, and the daughter of a mother lost, I have been tossed, bruised, and jostled into clarity about my idea of family. Now I know what I am willing to give, and to my birthdaughter it is a promise this time to stay; and to all of my children and their children, an unforgettable determination, which the writing of this book affirms, to end a legacy of leaving.

Giving Away Simone

Prologue

I never knew the details, but the story went something like this.

In 1934, my mother was born to Mavis Peabody and a man named John Thurgood.★ They were not married, and had no intentions to be, so Mavis's angry, embarrassed mother renounced her daughter and banished her from home.

With no place else to go, Mavis and her daughter, Ruth Ann, stayed at the hospital in Derry, New Hampshire, where the baby had been born. For a year Mavis earned room and board by working as a nurse's aid at the hospital. There she met Frances Cook,★ whose brother and his wife, Eddie and Altie Smith, were childless. The Smiths saw and fell in love with Ruth Ann. They wanted to adopt her.

By the time adoption papers were signed, Mavis had left Derry and was living in Dallas, Texas, where she had a job as a store clerk.

That was as much as my grandmother Altie H. Smith, the woman who had adopted my mother, knew.

And that is how, as far as I knew, this story began.

After years of wondering and a day of research, I have found and met Mavis Peabody, my eighty-five-year-old biological grandmother, the woman who gave away my mother. Mavis confirmed that her mother, Clara Jones, had disowned her—and that Clara herself had been abandoned by her mother, Sylvia Spears.

So our family tradition of mothers leaving their children had in fact begun in 1886, when Mavis's grandmother Sylvia had walked away from *her* daughter, and has thrived, like some noxious subterranean germ, for five generations. Maybe this blood-linked maternal trouble goes back even further. I don't know. But this is enough.

My biological daughter, Rebecca, the youngest in my family of the Separated, says we are here to kill the virus. I know she is right. I knew it the second I gave her away.

Part I

An Unnatural Act

1

I know exactly when it happened.

It was the creeping end of a restless afternoon of fingering forty-fives and playing with makeup (skin-clinging eyeliner and mouth-denying white lipstick) in the bathroom mirror of my grandmother's house. In my room, I popped and pushed to the downbeat of the Dells, undressing and dressing, replaying reels of my imagined night to come. Too much mascara, no bra, Jean Naté or not—I paced and waited for a wet-hot Friday night in August of 1968 to begin.

Finally, at five past six, I walked down a quarter mile of bumpy tar to Mim's Lunch to catch the six-twenty bus to Boston. Aproned women stepped from their houses to fan themselves with damp dish towels, and men sipped Moxie from tall plastic tumblers as they surveyed the ripening corn. It was the kind of summer night that pulls old people onto their cool, dark porches for the concert of hidden crickets. The thin fragrance from surviving patches of sweet fern still filled the air.

Inside Mim's, broad-backed men in snug, sun-bleached T-shirts sipped coffee, and squawking young families and old couples, for whom discourse was no longer necessary or interesting, feasted on fried clams, coleslaw, orange Crush, and sherbet. Waitresses in lacquered Grecian curls, lavender hanky corsages, and white-polished working shoes shuttled from booth to kitchen to booth with forearms full of dishes, their fixed faces softened only by the wink of a man at the counter wanting a refill.

I stood outside and waited, feeling like an alien nymph looking for transport to a secret planet, in a dress I had found in a drawer that hadn't been opened in years. It had been my mother's summer-thin, blue-striped dress that smelled of dusty, heated pine, and I was wearing it to Boston to see my boyfriend. I loved the way it buttoned in my breasts, how it fell off my hips, and curled in between my brown-summer legs when I walked. Wearing my mother's dress made me feel as if her arms were wrapping me up. But it made me miss her even more.

My boyfriend met me at the station in Boston, grabbed my waist with one arm, and didn't let go until we were underground at Park Street Station, on our way to the empty house of a friend whose parents were away at a car convention. We sat with our shoulders and thighs pressed into each other, rousing the current between us as the trolley lunged and jiggled out of the loud, roasting city into tree-shrouded stops, and our surroundings grew as quiet as we did. I looked at the far side of the aisle when I knew he was staring, feeling if our eyes met I would dissolve in a slow burn.

After twenty eternal minutes of climbing over rocks and hesitating under dead-end streetlamps, we found and entered the dark Victorian on a hill, and never turned on the lights.

Up the stairs on the second floor, moon shadows rippled across a broad, sheeted bed. We angled out of our clothes. From the second I began squeezing pearl buttons through the frayed slits in the front of my summer dress, I knew I was making dangerous moves. I backed onto the bed and spread my knees; he followed and hovered like a charged heat wave, long enough to look closely. I pulled hard on his shoulders, and gave my body to trouble (the kind, I was convinced, from which no mother—not even my mother—could walk away).

In the dense summer steam of the big house, I ruptured the quiet with longing—and then it was still. I ached from emptiness. I stumbled in the dark to find my soft dress and caught an early-morning bus while he still slept.

2

My grandmother Altie Hayes Smith would talk about "getting" my mother. "When we got her," she would say, sounding as if she'd been given a treasured appliance, "she was already walking." As a child I could not understand why anyone would want to give my mother away. My mother, joking, would say she couldn't understand it either. Such a beautiful baby. Imagine.

Little Ruth Ann was adopted at the unkind age of sixteen months and renamed Sara Eugena by the Smiths. My grandmother would tell stories about her newly acquired daughter's small-voiced pleas for a mama who wasn't her for months after the adoption. When I was young, there were vague references to my mother's natural mother, an unmarried woman, a good mother while her motherhood lasted, who had babies but kept giving them away.

Altie, my mother's new mother, was at her best when lesser folk were faint. She was a champ at funerals—she said all the right things, and with one brick-strong forearm could literally hold up a weak-kneed man. (When she made bread, she battered the dough so viciously we would step back, humbled by her jamming fists and the thrashing of the toughened heels of her hands.)

She was the one called into the houses of dead women by

husbands weak with grief, to sort out a wife's defunct clothing, erase the traces of sickness and death, praise the will of God, and deliver a week's worth of succotash, bread, and pie. She had delivered babies and bathed the dead with unflinching capableness.

Her husband deferred to his wife—except when he refused her apple pie, because, he would say for the zillionth time in forty-five years, he loathed it. "Thunderation, Eddie!" she would holler every time. "Since when?"

It was she who bought the Welch's grape juice and cut Wonder bread into wafers for communion for the fifty parishioners in her First Free Will Baptist Church, and she who cleaned, one by one, the purple-stained shot glasses after. My grandmother had a fifth-grade education but was a member of the school board (for the distinct purpose of advancing her school-aged daughter's interests), an officer in the Grange, the town clerk at one point, and grand matron in the Eastern Star (the female arm of the Masons). She lifted her full-bosomed trill in the church choir for four decades without missing a Sunday (except when she went to Florida for one week to visit an ailing sister-in-law), cooked bean suppers for groups of a hundred, and topstitched in the shoe shop for thirty-five years.

As an adult, my mother recalled feeling resentment of my grandmother's busy schedule, and her long working days, but she always said she felt lucky to have a mother so heroic, who would appear all-powerful against the enemy in a flash. When large, nine-year-old Barbara had bullied my mother one time too many in the schoolyard (she was irritated by my mother's double promotion and consistent A's), my grandmother made a personal visit to the home of the troublesome child. Altie appealed to Barbara's imagination by asking her to think how it would be if she, at five-foot-eight and 268 pounds, were to pull Barbara's hair, or push her off the swings at school. Barbara, word has it, trembled and promised peace. My mother happily recalled the story more than once.

As a child in the rural landscape of Benton, a small town an hour north of Boston, Sara loved wildflowers, swimming in the lake in summer, and her collie dog Champ, who bolstered her on the frozen lake in front of her house as she learned to ice skate and sat steadily in her boat as she fished for lake trout. She was surrounded by cousins, aunts, and uncles; her favorite was Uncle Gardner, who owned the general store, which entitled her to penny candy for the asking.

However, my mother's view of the country changed as she grew older; she began to see the New England that authors Edith Wharton *(Ethan Frome)* and Grace Metalious *(Peyton Place)* had portrayed with such bitterness. Metalious and Wharton wrote stories of betrayal, in which the safe promise of a small town's pretty, white-spired churches was slyly broken by the mean secrets and busy tongues of the worshipers within.

By the third grade, Sara Eugena was pondering the meaning of religion, taking an interest in history and politics and Cole Porter, and asking questions no one around her could answer; she began to use words (the ones she found in books) no one understood. Pictures of my mother from this period reveal a fine-featured, auburn-haired beauty, whose smile seems to have belonged to a delicate child of privilege. My mother grew affronted by the coarse strokes and petty boorishness of the bucolic, hardworking life provided by the Smiths. She didn't get their humor—in her view they were always laughing *at* people—and they never got hers (while on a fifth-grade library tour she had discovered Oscar Wilde).

As soon as Sara could read, she read everything she could find. Books were the doors through which she could travel out of her tiny town. When she was older, my mother seemed to take not only emotional but physical comfort from books, building encircling stacks of them wherever she sat, sticking dozens of feathered-paper strips to mark paragraphs worthy of revisiting, and writing comments and making check marks in the margins; she had a vigorous on-going dialogue with the pages within. She was reassured to have ideas and other worlds in sight, at arm's reach, the way Depression-era homemakers were comforted by an ever-present sack of flour: At least we won't starve, they would say.

By the end of fifth grade, my mother's teachers recommended she skip a grade (her IQ test results were the highest they'd seen). Altie and Sara's many aunts and uncles boasted about their smart relative, and how she would read a book a day given the chance. Yet Altie, who read only the Bible, could never come close to knowing the map of her daughter's mind; it was another world. As a child, my mother was crushed by what she felt was her mother's inability to have even the vaguest notion of who her only child was.

And Benton was a town unaccustomed to such precocity in its children, so Altie's daughter was especially vulnerable to the eddy of thin-lipped gossip. It was one thing to be suspiciously well-read at six, but too much to be of unknown and most likely contaminated origin. My grandmother knew enough about her town to tell her four-year-old that she was adopted, "before someone else did."

When Sara misbehaved, she recalled hearing neighbors and relatives murmur to each other, "I told Altie she shouldn't have gotten that girl. I knew she'd be nothing but trouble."

So my mother grew up in a town that didn't trust her for reasons she could not change. She began to feel like an orphan all over again.

As she got older, Sara and her mother began to battle. Sara felt as if she had to fight just to avoid being swallowed up by her domineering mother. "As a child, no one could tell me that women were weak or inferior and expect me to believe that," my mother once said. "Altie was the only person I ever really argued with, but I always respected her."

By the age of eleven, my mother had read too much about independent thinking—most memorably Thomas Paine—to agree to be baptized. (Baptists wait until their worshipers are pubescent to enact their ablution. The more proximate to burgeoning sexuality, they must figure, the more effective the cleansing.) Altie was aghast. But the visiting English vicar supported my mother's decision to forgo baptism, explaining she had a right to her opinion (thus accounting, she has said, for her enduring affection for all things British), and Sara escaped the bath. My mother considered this standoff her first official victory in her mother-daughter war.

My father, a twenty-seven-year-old tennis coach at a girls' camp in the next town over, said he first noticed my mother one summer as she rode by on her bike when she was ten. He was struck by her poise and knowing smile. He asked someone from the town where she was from. "Who knows?" smirked my mother's neighbor as he waved his hand, dismissing her, even though he knew she was Altie Smith's adopted daughter.

Five summers later, on a late August afternoon, Sara rode her bike again up Bellmay Road and at the town's softball game spotted the man who had noticed her years before. In recalling her first vision of him, she remembered his tanned back through the glistening chain-link fence, as he stood on deck, swinging a bat into the sun. He happened to turn and see her. At that moment, she said later, she fell in love. He smelled of cities, places she hadn't been.

When my mother, barely sixteen and pregnant, wanted to drop out of high school to marry this man who was twice her age, my grandmother drew up the guest list without skipping a beat. She shopped for and bought a lacy white gown for her engaged daughter, sent out seventy-five Hallmark invitations, booked her Baptist minister for the third Saturday in May, and decorated a four-tiered cake she had baked from six boxes of Duncan Hines mix.

After the wedding, my mother moved into my father's four-bedroom house in a suburb of Boston and awaited the birth of her first biological relative, due the second week of November 1950. Two weeks after her son was born, she was pregnant again, and, in September of 1951, I was born.

3

For the first ten years the four of us—my parents, my brother, and I—spoke freely and laughed often. We absorbed our mother's boundless, spirited intelligence and were amused by our father's eccentricities. We were the indigent aristocracy, Bohemians in the 'burbs, house rich, penny poor.

My frugal father, whose professional passion was jazz, had inherited from his parents a house and enough blue-chip stocks to yield an ascetic living. Once and briefly, in a noble attempt to be a Head of Household (a father and husband's commission in the fifties), he took a desk job, for which he reluctantly wore a tie and coat (both 1930s versions, which he had retrieved from his late father's closet). After two effortful months, there seemed to be a collective surrender in our house to the inevitability that my father's attempt at convention was not to last. Though he never complained, and every night after work brought home Bazooka bubble gum or Red Hots for my brother and me, his sluggish smiles made it clear that early rising, suit jackets, and daily work were an ill fit. My mother was happy to have him back.

Aside from a part-time job with late-morning hours in a shoe store (arranged by a family friend), my father never again tackled a full day's worth of work. (One of the benefits of my father's job in the Bass shoe store was free footwear for his

family. I walked around in brown-tie oxfords for years without a say and drooled at the patent-leather, pearl-broached
slip-ons my friends wore on Sundays.)

My mother never insisted my father find ambition. She,
who would never allow herself to be the pestering wife ("it
is *so* common"), assumed, as he did of her, that she could
count on her husband to do what made him happy.

My father's plan for providing for his family on a meager
interest income was to play poker often and well (which
regularly yielded grocery money), to refrain from costly habits
(he never smoked and drank only the one drink provided
gratis at his music gigs), and to make clear his vicious contempt for waste. His spending habits were vigorously guided
by the tenet of the old-monied: Never touch the principal.
We never had health or home insurance, and medical, especially dental, bills sent him reeling.

He fined my brother and me five cents when we failed to
clean our teeth (he checked toothbrushes for recent water
drops). My friend Lorraine said she never knew food came in
such small containers until she visited our pantry one day, and
saw two four-ounce tuna cans and a half-size ketchup bottle.
In the winter—to fight the high cost of heat—my father
would shuffle to the breakfast table in his World War II olive
wool coat while we shivered over our Cheerios. My mother
would sit on her double-socked feet as she wrapped her
fingers around another steaming cup of coffee (in between
breaking Lucky Strikes in half so a pack would last longer).
My brother and I never knew a leftover until we left home.

My mother, on the other hand, was both reasonable and
generous with the money she eventually made from part-time
jobs. In contrast to my father's tightly managed, invisible
money, my mother's pocketbook sat on the floor next to her
chair, always agape, often revealing a small bouquet of dollars

and loose change. What little she had, it was understood, we were welcome to. However, consideration, as in all matters, was expected.

For many years, we agreed our father was amazing. He played the piano by ear and could tell time to the minute without a watch. He located our lost things (most often my glasses) by phoning the mythological Blue Bunny. We were proud of his frivolous triumphs—in addition to poker, he played tennis and pool and flew kites the best we had ever seen.

Our parents made serious work of telling us often how wanted we both were, how specifically their wishes for children, one of each, had been fulfilled.

As my brother and I grew older, both our parents spoke openly of their disdain for the institution of marriage. My father cut out and kept taped to the dining room wall a Voltaire quotation: "Marriage is the deathbed of love," until it turned crisp and yellow with age. Marriage killed the romance, he said. He would have preferred part-time cohabitation, which would leave enough hours in his week to read, play jazz and tennis, cuddle his cats in the sun, and leisurely trim his lawn.

My mother refused to be called Mrs. Waldron. You can call me Sara, she would firmly advise my friends, some of whom had been so strictly trained to address a wife and mother by the proper title that they couldn't quite permit themselves the informality.

I was never Daddy's Little Girl. Most of the time I felt like Dad's independent charge, whose individuality was granted at birth. He taught me how to catch hardballs and how to bowl and had little regard for how I should look, though he was sure he didn't understand dresses. ("Not very practical, I would think.'') My father and my mother had no plans about the future paths of their children, other than their expectation of each other—that we would do what made us happy.

There was rarely enough food, but there always seemed to be money for lessons. Our parents provided tennis, ballet, boxing, and piano lessons, museum visits, no TV, precise manners, and a work ethic to enable us to freely traverse class lines should we choose to do so. We enjoyed a limitless social frontier as kids—blissfully unranked by what we owned or by the work our parents did (or did not do, as the case seemed to be).

Our parents weren't about to contrive with the masses in the usual observance of most holidays. We were told that a Santa Claus did not exist but were firmly advised about keeping the truth to ourselves. Most children believe in these things, my mother warned, and it's not up to you to break the news. Instead, Christmas became a month-long festival of food and crafts, an active pageant of the senses. We made things—cookies, ornaments, candles, macaroni wreaths, juniper boughs cum bows—and we stenciled everything. My mother dipped wintergreen mints in chocolate and made a St. Lucy's ring, an elaborate circle of pastry, French in origin, to decorate the first tier of our dining room buffet. Swedish straw reindeer leaned into each other on the mantel, and the twelve days of Christmas, squares of felt that my mother had patiently hand-cut in multicolored detail, adorned the woodwork between rooms.

As scant as our family was—there were no aunts, uncles, or cousins because our parents were sibling free—our house bustled during the holidays, especially after my grandparents Altie and Eddie arrived. Nana, as I always called Altie, kept the house going while my mother snuck away to put the last of the gold bric-a-brac on our Christmas stockings or finish a hand-knit sweater. My father and grandfather played cribbage.

When I was eleven, my mother gave me a small enveloped edition of Dylan Thomas's *A Child's Christmas in Wales.* I didn't open it for weeks because I was almost sure it wouldn't suit me. But then my mother asked me to read it to her. And I did. From that point on, when I first read of "the few small aunts . . . like faded cups and saucers," the useless presents, including "many-colored jelly-babies," I began to find words delicious, possessed of a rare power. In the next week I started to write a contrived and fairly senseless "novel" on the backs of dozens of pieces of scrap paper, which I showed my father and which he dutifully read and encouraged.

Church was forbidden by my parents, even against my early pleas (occasional urges for the traditional life eventually passed); my father was an atheist, my mother, an ex-Baptist agnostic, and they wanted their children to grow free from the guilty imprint and passivity they were sure institutionalized religion guaranteed.

Our apparent lack of a spiritual life, however, troubled our neighbors. Well-meaning men of the cloth knocked at our pagan door more than once and greeted my mother and father with solemn pleas—certainly you must know the perils of a churchless childhood, they implored. (My mother knew only the unbearable dread of Bible School three times a week and twice on Sundays, and, regrettably, the perverse lust of a certain visiting minister.) My father thought the religious foolish and cowardly. But our neighbors persisted. They were convinced that what our family was missing, besides a television set and Coca-Cola, was the presence of Jesus. My parents swiftly but politely sent these eager men of God on their way.

As often as our family was suspected, it was, oddly, cited for

its civilized offspring; there was no disputing the good manners and unusual intelligence of the hardworking Waldron
kids. Our neighbors the Tillistons would shake their heads at
the number and difficulty of our chores; and it is true, my
brother and I did laundry, washed dishes, vacuumed, and
made our own school lunches starting in the first grade. My
brother ironed clothes as often as I emptied the trash; the
division of labor was not gender-specific, and I enjoyed no
daughterly exemptions from dirty work.

This vigorous approach to engendering self-reliance at a
young age—a combination of our parents' laziness in matters
of household maintenance and a commitment on their part to
raise children devoid of same—resulted occasionally in gross
lunches and bad dress. I remember concocting a special school
lunch, a peanut butter and Hershey syrup sandwich, for a
picnic our second-grade class had planned. By the time I had
reached the schoolyard tree that afternoon, my sandwich had
turned into a bruised, edemic, inedible pancake. I was too
embarrassed to explain why I was lunchless, ditched the sandwich, and sipped warm milk in the shade while other kids ate
neat bologna sandwiches and Oreo cookies that had been
perfectly wrapped by mothers in aprons.

Nonetheless my mother would get calls from the parents of
shy or impolite children, imploring her to divulge the secrets
of her mothering; and do you think my daughter and yours
could play together? My mother left that up to me. The Loop
sisters, three round-nosed, minuscule, elderly women who
crowded into their second-story living room picture window
to monitor, shamelessly, our house, complimented my
mother regularly and called on her for help in influencing, if
she could, the ornery kids on Lamont Street who could not
seem to respect their elders; and while they were at it, wasn't
the light in my brother's room a bit dim for studying?

Every year until we were ten, about a week before school ended, my brother and I were dropped off at our grandmother's house in the New Hampshire country for what seemed an eternal stretch of placid days. We would make the two-hour trip on old roads, stopping once on the way for black raspberry ice cream and playing car games in teams—my father and brother against my mother and me. I remember feeling so content that I thought I would burst.

My mother wore lipstick and a rarely seen cotton shirtwaist dress with rhinestone buttons and chocolate poppies in celebration of our annual late-June trip north, and my father wore his it-must-be-summer orange sherbet shirt. My brother and I, grateful to be sprung prematurely from the last restless days of school, crouched amid fat suitcases in the backseat of our '52 Chevy in clean shorts and Keds.

As a kid I loved Benton. Swimming in the lake until blind with hunger, picking corn from the garden for supper, gobbling an endless supply of pies, blueberry muffins, strawberry shortcake, and candy bars. In the late morning, after a heavy breakfast of French toast, poached eggs, and bacon, my brother and I would walk to the general store to buy comic books, *Betty and Veronica* for me and *Spider-Man* for him. In the afternoons we helped our grandmother set the table at the town hall for Saturday bean suppers, climbed trees, or caught crayfish from the banks of the Double-S River. One summer I practiced smoking my great-uncle Franny's stolen Newport menthol cigarettes in the shed with an older girl, who gave me detailed lessons on how to inhale and later showed me secrets under the sheets.

Mostly, we belonged to our grandmother for the summer—our parents returned often and for weeks at a time to Boston. My grandmother would've kept us forever. Once she took us to the drive-in movie seven miles away—she had finally relented—only to find the feature starred a minimally clothed Brigitte Bardot, who proceeded to undress for a series of smitten lovers. My brother and I, in pajamas in the back, giggled and whispered, while my grandmother kept to herself in the front, her big hands holding her purse tighter by the minute on top of her overcoated lap, hoping we understood nothing, never daring to look back.

While the childhood within our family was out of the mainstream, the outside world of my fifties youth was grounded in convention. Our childhood view of the world was reinforced at the edges by characters out of central casting from a previous era, on the cusp of the modern world. There were gentle bridges between generations when I was young, and the spotty but memorable presence of old people served as surety for a kid worried about life's permanence.

On Saturdays we went to the Fairmount Theatre to see movies that scared us. Next door, Tony, an old, bald Italian man with a pure white mustache who wore a white wrap-around apron up to his fleshy chest, kept his soda fountain/candy store open despite an obvious customer disinterest. He lowered his head as he pushed in slow motion a broom across his wooden floor in half darkness and tried to chase wiseass kids out of his place when they stole fireballs from the glass bins on top of the marble counter. His bad eyesight and hearing made him sport. Tony didn't seem to care that he never caught anyone. He would sell an ice cream to the kid he knew had stolen a stick of licorice the Saturday before.

There was Chickie the ice cream man, a retired cabbie, whose flat, creased face hosted a bobbing, half-ash cigarette as he told us stories about kids who were maimed for life because they licked their Popsicles too soon after he had taken them out of his banana-colored refrigerated truck. "Lost his tongue. Like that. The whole tongue."

And our pediatrician, Dr. Munroe, a heavy, firm-footed woman in her early seventies whose attendant was the nicer half of her Boston marriage. In the blurry background of my memory are the ragmen inching down the street in greasy trucks and the icemen hauling their frigid loads.

4

Though I was always aware that we resided on the irreligious fringe in our Catholic/Congregationalist community, our mother gave us enough of a sense of ourselves that we did not feel compelled to seek it elsewhere. Sara, however, had been sentenced to the outskirts from birth, without a sure idea of who she was. In our suburban neighborhood she found comfort, if temporarily, in the company of "individuals"—other sorts who resided outside, to the left most often, of center.

She played cards with men, wore jeans (when everyone else's mother was wearing shirtwaists, hose, and pearls), read *Esquire* magazine for men, Mary McCarthy, and books about the ancient history of Rome. She was friends with the adult sons of the one Jewish family in our neighborhood, and became a confidante to the gay son of a local politician. In her twenties, my mother had made something of a salon of our house, and we, the children, were accustomed to vehement discussion, raucous wit, late-night adult card games, and the background scat of Ella Fitzgerald—and occasionally the groggy body of our father's drummer stretched out in rumpled clothes on the couch downstairs the next morning.

My mother was out of step in the tradition-clutching postwar years. She scrutinized politics, devoured books, and was keenly aware of social trends. She stayed attuned to the emotional lives of her friends and family, and their friends too. But no one went as fast as she did. No one, it seemed, could keep up or go as far, see as quickly or clearly or feel as deeply. The more frantic her perceptions, the lonelier her life became. As her children approached adolescence, my mother's inner mind and outer life came to be at odds, starkly, achingly out of sync. There were friends, but no one, not even her protective, admiring friend Marsha, also an adoptee, could touch or soothe the isolation that had begun in the extreme when she was so young and that continued to overtake her as she grew older. Losing her mother at an age when she was old enough to know it was a memory that never stopped hurting her.

My father started to back away when my brother and I began to need more from him than a playing partner and his marriage required a higher grade of commitment—the long-lasting kind. His own solitary childhood had left him unprepared for the challenge of going with his family into a second decade of intimacy.

He had been told by his championship bridge-playing mother and her devoted husband more than once, and bluntly, that he was an unplanned child. My father's grandmother, who lived with him, provided what little communication and affection he recalled as an adult. They talked about movies and sports, and she alone kissed him good night. My father never spoke about his parents to me until a month before he died, and then he said, in response to my prodding, that he could not remember ever having been hugged by either of them.

After ten years of marriage, my father began to stay out all night after his jazz gigs. He'd sleep all day and would be fixing his breakfast in his bathrobe as my brother and I returned home from school. He tuned out our lives and began to function as if he were living alone (he had *his* glass, *his* towel, *his* ice cream). My mother told me then she felt as if she could not reach him; she had tried, she said, gritting her teeth, but he was not there.

Each sadness or letdown seemed to compound her internal homelessness. For the woman who feels and thinks too much before her allowable time, being alone becomes a customary sentence; for a young woman whose mother had originated the sentence, it was enough to make a mind go AWOL.

As my brother and I, at the ages of twelve and eleven, began to edge out of our home into our circle of friends (as is the wont of growing kids), and as her husband retreated, my mother sensed the inevitability of being abandoned, again. In a scene I will never forget, I spoke what must have been a confirmation of her worst fears.

One night I called her from the office of a children's theater I was involved with and in which I had found a core of close friends with whom I had begun to spend most of my free time. I had called to ask if I could stay in town, past dark, to go for pizza. No, she said, she didn't want me in the city so late. I snapped back, nastily, "You're just holding on because your kids are all you have." She hung up on me. I was instantly, miserably sorry for what I had said—and wanted to call her back, to retract it. But I didn't. It was a deep under-the-skin gouge, because, in a way, it was true. I was playing my ace. We, her only biological relatives, her truest family whom she had dared to love so closely, were about to replay the curse of her original relative: We were beginning our exodus from home, from her. So horrifying was the thought of being left—even in the usual adolescent increments—that she would do whatever it took to stop it.

And so, as she approached thirty, as her children were getting ready to leave and her husband was losing interest in his marriage, my mother began a descent that had left her intolerant of much more than isolation—a continuing state not happier for her but I suspect overall easier, and cruelly familiar. Her perceptions had become so blinding, her senses so raw, that being alone, away from the perceptible lives of others (especially those she loved), became an act of self-preservation. She could not know that her children were not leaving for good; or that we were not leaving at all, merely stepping out, that we'd be back. She could not bear her husband's retreat. The scent of rejection, no matter how slight or temporary, forecast for her unbearable emotional danger. This time, she would impose the isolation, before we could.

5

My mother's world, as she had begun to see it, was engorged with pain; so she created another.

She would sit by the phone inside the wide maroon wings of an old chair with the lights out, dialing strangers, smirking without obvious cause. Her lips and skin became parched, and her once warm eyes grew colorless; her body became a weary tomb to be rearranged unwillingly inside the small cove of her dark chair—the station of her unwinding.

The murky woodwork, thin Oriental carpets, and lightlessness of the house we lived in had always spooked me (resulting in an adult tendency to decorate with pastels and a preference for undressed windows). As a little girl, after our nightly Uncle Wiggily chapter, I would step hesitantly up and away from the dark, dusty corners of the stained oak stairs to my bed in the dark, keeping an eye on my calm mother until I could race into my room and shut the door. Now, with the unpredictable tenancy of my faltering mother, the house became a dungeon of terrible surprises. She made barricades around her chair and would curl up inside amid several weeks' worth of newspaper dunes, magazines, coffee cups, tissues, and heaping ashtrays. When we could not stand it, my brother and I threw out the papers. My father did not come out of his room.

She wrote, wildly, pages and pages, which she sent off as letters to imagined lovers or perceived conspirators. Her eyes glazed over, and she would break into a smile, as if she were recalling an unforgettable euphoria. I would ask, nervously, why she was smiling, and she would laugh and say nothing. She took to her room, separate from my father's, and weakly mothered us from bed amid open books, coffee cups, and letters she hadn't yet sent. After school I hurried home to the foot of her bed and tried nervously to coax lucidity from her. But she stopped touching me and drifted further from us each day. I could only watch, a paralyzed voyeur, as my mother, on the edge of her mind, became, finally, a shadow.

During this time, my brother and I were moved to my mother's best friend's house for several weeks. Marsha Sweat would take care of us while we went to school, make our lunches, and see to it that we had clean clothes. She did not talk about our mother. We couldn't go home, we were told, because our mother would not be there. She was at a hospital, but we were not told why. And my brother and I never asked, but we knew it was bad enough to be unsayable.

The weeks we spent at Marsha's house were an awful limbo of darkness (it must've been winter), awkward quiet, and throbbing sadness. Where was our father? Would our mother come back? Was she all right? I wanted to know; but I missed my mother so much I could not speak.

When we finally went home, we were told our mother would be tired and needed her rest. But *I* needed *her*. For weeks after her return, I inspected her from the far end of the room in which she dozed, or stood motionless and quiet around the corner where she sat and stared, and waited for her to want me back. I carefully listened to her every utterance, even though I didn't want to hear what she might say. I was both transfixed and repelled by the lifeless stranger my mother had become; I could not take my eyes off her.

In the weeks after her return home, I began to feel for the first time that she no longer loved me like crazy (as I had always felt when she was well). Now sometimes I feel it would've been far better for me to have lost her to instant physical death. I could've gotten mad, sad, and gone on. Instead, at eleven, I began a long, frightened vigil, always hoping for the return of the mother I knew, helpless to make it happen. Over the next few months, our father gradually explained why our mother had gone away. She had had a nervous breakdown, he said, which meant her mind wasn't right, and she needed help.

After about a year of housebound lethargy, my mother emerged from her brittle chrysalis, energized by her rancor, as a bitter despot, strident and distant, judging and dismissing the people she loved, alienating everyone else. She accused my brother, her husband, and me of conspiring against her, of joining "the street theater" in devising a plan to control her every move, even the words that came out of her mouth. This amorphous league, and its considerable membership, was accountable for all her unhappiness. If she cried, her tears were the political plan of another and certainly not from her own sadness. She mocked the ambition, confidence, and openness she had once encouraged in me, accused me of "masquerading, like the others." She was not, she confided, pleased with my brother's fake opinions and bourgeois pose.

Still believing, above all else, that my mother could not lie, I approached my friends as her advocate, shaming them for being part of the System that tormented her.

"You don't know it yet," I warned, "but you are part of

this." The humiliation I may have felt with friends when the truth was known was inconsequential compared with the horror I felt when I realized that her wise mind had grown sick, and that I could no longer believe my mother.

No one was safe. She could track down one's weak spot with savage accuracy, push her imagined enemies up against the wall into the white flash of a floodlight, and watch them squirm, despising their inability to scratch back. She became masterful at bringing out the worst in those around her, transforming especially those she loved into stammering, regretfully confused defendants. The damage she seemed to want to do was a measure of her hurt, leaving the ambushed unbearably sad for knowing this and inexpressibly angry at having been drawn into the maelstrom of her pain. She became idea stricken, singularly intellectual and critical, steering clear of emotion, the felt sense. Gone were my mother's smiles, her gentle strokes and warm humor. I had relied on her instincts from one day of my childhood to the next, and now they were buried in the chill of dogma.

My mother used to say her children's good behavior was a result of her having created a world within her family. Inclusion in this familial place, to be "a Waldron," was made to feel so exclusive and desirable that one complied with the rules without question, in order to belong. Conforming behavior (good manners, generosity, humor, and critical thought) was a comparatively small fee for such privileged membership. Guided by a well mind and a generous spirit, residing in our world within the world felt both cozy and exciting.

But when my mother got sick, the message about membership grew vindictive: You're out if you sully, even slightly, the family mystique. The hazing requirements, constant evaluation of one's character while in her company, intensified. The world my mother created became a place in which she could never be rejected because she was its founder, judge, and gatekeeper. So intensely had my mother wanted a world of her own, a universe which would not cast her out, that she brilliantly spun one into existence—in which membership was conditional for everyone but her.

I have often thought how my well mother would have loathed the woman she had become; how she would've grabbed her kids and run from this mean-spirited monster.

It was during this time that she announced her unwillingness to be referred to as Mum, as my brother and I had always called her. From now on, she would be known as Sara by her twelve- and thirteen-year-old children. At first, probably because it was the antiauthority midsixties, this wholesale trashing of parental labels was a stylish aberration. Even then, shortly after my mother abdicated her parenthood, we grinned at the pro forma lack of familial convention.

But now I see another motivation in her deliberate announcement to retire from her place of authority. Transforming her identity from mother to peer, she may have thought, might discourage her teenagers' predictable mutiny. When we were on the brink of rebellion, she bailed out of motherhood. Kids rebel against mothers, after all, not relatives known on a first-name basis.

Now I miss what the word assumes, though as a forty-two-year-old daughter I forget how it feels to use the word, and the world of two it reveals. Sometimes I say the word out loud when I'm alone, to see if reminders will rush in. But it has been too long. I feel nothing. Mum. Chum. Chad. Mum. But when my sons call me Mum, it is careful music to me; it is our repeated, rhapsodic understanding.

★ ★ ★

When my mother got ill and my father grew disabled as a parent and husband, never knowing, it seemed, what to say to his growing children nor to his deluded wife, our family became unhinged. My mother did not admit and has never acknowledged her illness, so she never considered seeking help and turned mean when it was suggested. My father had not bargained for the aging complexity of my mother's mind (she was a teenager when they married), so with hidden hurt he blamed her for her tattered autonomy, eventual collapse, and ultimately her failure to continue to be his wife.

Once, during a bad week, as an adolescent warrior in the quiet war that was our home, I looked in the yellow pages for help and saw an ad for Family Services. I called and made an appointment and took my brother with me into the city. We sat, edgy but righteous, across from a wide, blue-suited woman who informed us, with spirited condescension, that at least one parent, an adult, would have to be present to file a report. But, we whispered, embarrassed, they won't. She was sorry, she said, there was nothing they could do.

The adults had checked out, embittered by their own losses. We, the children, grew closer over the next three years in a bunker of sibling support amid the shock waves of a ripped up family. Being near my brother made all the difference then. For me, only my brother's company could cure the brutalizing loneliness of our mother's fury. We knew the same disturbing house quiet, and we could decode the doublespeak our mother mumbled on her bad days. We could tell a bad day within seconds—in the morning she would begin with bitter stares and short sentences, as if we had committed a crime against her in our sleep the night before. We mocked our father's desperate silence and loafed within the dangerous cage that was our house.

During the days leading up to the dissolution of our family, my brother and I would hole up in his room, lie across his bed, and smoke cigarettes. We would mouth the lyrics of the godly Dylan and chuckle sourly at the Stones' version of "Nineteenth Nervous Breakdown" as we did algebra assignments or made up obscene Latin idioms instead of translating Gallic Wars or declining verbs. We never got enough sleep, and our schoolwork suffered; we tried to stay away at the houses of friends when possible. We lived on frozen pizza and cereal, earnings from my brother's part-time library job and my baby-sitting.

My mother wanted a divorce. She became enraged at my father for giving up and going away. My father passively relented, bitterly hurt by his wife's collapse. She contacted a lawyer about it, but my brother and I handled most of the divorce business thereafter; we made and showed up for appointments, informed the attorney about the state of our parents' marriage (my father was not buying food, he had seemed especially mean to our mother the week before, there was no money for school lunches), and located documents when necessary. Our attorney seemed to have a protective admiration for my brother's and my part in this adult business of divorce; but, in a horrifying lapse of good judgment, he asked my brother to testify against our father in court—to advance our case—and, regrettably, my brother at fifteen, for the sake of his mother, did.

Our parents had defaulted, leaving my brother and me to act as sole guardians of each other's growing.

In the midst of our family decline, my brother moved to my grandparents' house in the country. Left behind, I started packing up my youth, readying for the worst. I dropped out of my favorite school, Girls' Latin. For years after leaving GLS in my junior year, I had dreams that haunted me for the rest of the day. I was back at school in my senior year, among friends and familiar teachers in a sunny, wooden room, getting ready to graduate. Together we had survived the rigors of our beloved academe and were at last gathered in warm, triumphant conclusion. Then I would awaken, realizing that I hadn't finished and that I would never graduate from GLS.

I will always remember the huge, stone-carved statues of Greek goddesses who monitored the halls of my old school. Minerva, draped in toga and laurels, had guarded with calm the entrance to our guidance counselor Miss Glennon's office; and Artemis, oozing valor, stood on the landing to the second floor. I used to like seeing her after I came out of chemistry class, where the large and very cranky Miss Lord would, yet again, have exposed my inability to understand anything scientific.

Miss Willard, whom I was sure I would refer to as Miss Walrus eventually because of her striking resemblance to some heavy, beached mammal, had red hair piled into a peak above her fleshy face. She knew everything about literature but spoke so slowly and saw so badly that we used to mouth the ends of her sentences before she did. She encouraged discussion, listened well, so we talked, debated, and discussed everything in her English class. Miss Mannix, lover of Shakespeare, would ask, "Do we have an opinion, girls?" at least seven times per class and would insist on a thinking girl's answer.

Mr. Campbell, my Latin teacher, had bushy eyebrows and an uneven gray crew cut, thick lips always smiling over big, sharp teeth, and his suits, shirts, and ties were rarely pressed or clean. He was one of only two men in our all-girls school and seemed to work especially hard at proving how gentle and chivalrous the other gender could be. He told us where the best places to ice-skate were, informed us about perfect tomato sauce, and occasionally taught us some Latin, but overall he could waste fifty minutes better than anyone we knew, and we were grateful for him. In late autumn of my freshman year, Mr. Campbell had a heart attack. It was the first time anyone who mattered to me had died, and I walked slowly and fought tears for weeks after.

Celeste was my best friend in school. We shared a raspberry lime rickey with two straws at Brigham's after school whenever one of us had leftover lunch money. She took German, and I took French. I hated the guttural sound of German, and she razzed me about the silly softness of French. She was obsessed with Jack Kerouac. Together we complained about the work we had to do, loathed Miss MacNamera, laughed about Miss Walrus, and mourned Mr. Campbell. I missed her most when I left.

Being in our house during the final months of my parents' marriage had become an impossible fight against the slow decay that was eating our family. I discussed my decision to leave my school with no one. No one was home. My father was in his room; my mother had grown more distant by the day, and my brother was gone. I was left only with the enclosed forum of my head in which to bounce the pros and cons. I simply announced I would be leaving. I think my parents said okay.

I figured I couldn't or shouldn't expect to cope with the demands of Girls' Latin School on top of everything else. I wanted to scale down the challenges before me. Or so I thought. Now I think I was looking for a resounding, protective parental insistence on staying at the good school where I had found success.

The fact is, I needed my school then more than ever. In the mornings I would fumble through our dark, messy house as my parents slept, gather my books, scavenge for lunch money, and sleepily ride two buses and one trolley to GLS. When I arrived at school, the dreariness of home fell away. Sanity and order prevailed. Each day, in the first few minutes before the bell rang, I became gradually transplanted in purpose.

I could have continued knee-deep in dusty classics and Latin declensions, in the company of girlfriends and devoted teachers, but instead I declared I would leave GLS, hoping someone would talk me out of it. My father drove me to my school on a January day in 1967 to sign withdrawal papers. My headmistress, visibly disappointed, implored me and my father to think more about this decision; I was a good student and had come so far. But my father stood awkwardly silent between us. Then she shook my hand and said good-bye, and I said nothing too.

After I dropped out of Girls' Latin, I went to our local high school, where the teachers seemed more concerned with the bad manners of the boys than with the fact that I could translate French sentences reasonably well or that I had an opinion about Hawthorne. What I had come to consider my good qualities (thoughtfulness, humor, and quickness) were not redeemable in this coed environment. What was, compliance and coyness, I didn't have or didn't want. With my family life spiraling downward and my school days filled with defeat, Girls' Latin School seemed kinder by the day and irretrievably distant, like a lifeboat growing smaller on the horizon and finally indecipherable (except in my dreams).

I could have kept at least one happy regimen, my familiar academia, but instead I blew the odds and cleared the decks for disaster.

6

In an inspired finale, during our last week at home before the divorce, my mother gleefully lit a brief bonfire in the driveway next to my father's coddled pink-tinged hollyhocks. Into it she fed his threadbare bathrobe—the one, she thought, he wore too often and far too late into the day. The week before she had gone on a credit-card spending spree, the cost of which surpassed by thousands the total sum of her meager marital allowance over the past seventeen years. She was not unhappy to be free from marriage.

After the divorce, my father settled gratefully into solitary living, in the house in which he had lived as a boy and we had lived until the divorce, but which would always be just his.

My mother and I moved into the city and rented a two-room walk-up. She stayed in bed, and I took an hour-long train ride back to the high school in my old neighborhood and worked from three to eleven most days in a hospital for the terminally ill to make our money. But when the divorce settlement came through, seven months later, my mother took off on a Greyhound cross-country bus tour with more money in her pocket than she had ever had. I was left, alone, to finish the last weeks of my junior year in high school.

★   ★   ★

The one who makes an early exit, of course, has the mercy of distant memory on her side and leaves us, the abandoned, wanting more. The image of one's absent mother, though assaulted intermittently and most likely subconsciously by the children left behind, not only withstands the test of time but blooms beyond the borders and resides, ultimately, in a colossal mental shrine into which much yearning is fed. We the deserted do not blame our mutinying mothers for leaving. We blame ourselves for not keeping them, absorbing the shame of our blighted families, granting amnesty to and making excuses for our wayward mothers. Orphaned children contrive images of suffering saints, heroes even, who had no choice, even if they did. The memory of the long-gone mother collects more gilt than dust. That is how much we need our mothers.

Deprived of my mother, I too have decided to treat myself to the most poetic memories I have of her. These mental pictures appear as a lilting mosaic of maroons and muted browns. I call them up for comfort.

I will always see her, white-skinned and fragile in a mahogany room lit by summer dusk, in a sea of books and smoke. Or holding me on her lap on the stairs, her mouth on my cheek, whispering, her perfect oval nails over my arm, amid the scent of lotion and tobacco. Or the bittersweet moment when I would watch her press coral lipstick onto her full lips, up close to the kitchen mirror under the amber light, knowing she would leave when she was done.

I will remember how she illuminated boundless possibilities for me. I think of the conscious generosity with which she approached the rearing of a daughter, when she was barely out of her teens, as she struggled to invent her own soul. She gave me the troublesome Eloise (to be admired) at the Plaza when I could barely read; Susan B. Anthony as an idea for a report ("a woman for a change") in the fourth grade; and *The Second Sex* by Simone de Beauvoir on my twelfth birthday (stressing to me the part about de Beauvoir's painful regret at not having had children; my mother found the thought unbearable). She encouraged me to think outside the usual ambitions ("How about an idea-man in advertising?" she suggested).

Some of her insights will never leave me: Trust your instincts. Anger is good. Have an opinion, articulate it, be prepared to defend it. Nothing is that serious. Share your good thoughts. Human relations are far more important than all else. She had been an intimate observer of her children, and as an adoptee was palpably ecstatic at having had us, her first biological relatives. She gave us all of her, and saw her motherhood as royal work. As her young daughter I felt free to be my essential self without payment.

When I was a girl, it was often said that I bore an uncanny resemblance to my mother. Introductions were instantly and predictably followed by the beaming, head-shaking adult uttering, "Don't you look *just* like your mother?" For the adoptee who looks like no one for so long, a reflection in the form of a relative provides a unique comfort, and my mother had been granted a daughter whose image was a familial match in the extreme. But I wanted to be an original, to look like myself. I was annoyed by what must have been for my mother a truly satisfying moment. Yet for years after the inevitable comparison was made, with a charity I sensed even then, she would find my eyes and whisper, "But much prettier."

So extreme was the change in our home after our family fell apart that, as an adult, I began referring to my childhood as Part One and Part Two; the latter a nightmarish paradox of the former. But it was the gift of my mother's presence in my early childhood that nourished me as much as the pain of her absence haunted me in the later years. I cannot imagine not having had that time with her, the warm-flesh-of-her-lap-and-scented-hands days, being near the slow roundness of her woman body, the body that I am becoming and that I love for its loyalty to my memory of hers.

Without our years together, given as though my mother knew she couldn't make it last, as armament against the years to follow, I am certain I would be afloat, searching feverishly for terra firma, contriving a past that could nourish or help in some way to soften a disjointed future. Her eyes whose color I share, our similar walks and laughs reassure me of where I began being, in her, near her, and allow me to assume my lovability. I cannot imagine living without that steady memory of origin, the fact of my wanted beginning.

My friend Lorraine often escaped to our house from the violence in her own family to sit near my mother at our dining room table to feel safe and be understood. My mother paid attention to my brother's friends, asked their opinions. She took carloads of adolescent kids to the beach, to the country, on day trips to the airport, and she took them seriously. She drove and listened, advised and observed; she was our respectful guardian, who was slowly but secretly fading. Nobody, it would become clear later, had been giving or listening to her all this time. And she did not dare ask. By the time she had reached her late twenties, my mother had not reasonably measured how much she could give and still save enough for herself.

7

In the month before my mother left, I met a man I'd seen playing guitar in the park nearly every day; he never let a conversation or his music making impede his bodacious scanning of female walkers-by. He was black and probably twice my age. Instead of turning away from his stare, I decided to sink into it.

Sixties social mores had deemed African-American men haute couture. The cultural elite courted angry black men, Leonard Bernstein partied with Black Panthers; to be radical, as Tom Wolfe wrote, was to be chic. The integration of black street culture with white parlor society now appears as a fickle fashion statement rather than a lasting political mandate, as blacks struggle, at the end of this century, to survive under a pall of self-loathing and political invisibility. But back then, the alabaster hands of monied white women could often be seen wrapped around the dashikied ebony arms of men cashing in on a brief, titillating moment in the sociopolitical sun.

The man who became my lover was glad to be paraded, but I didn't know how or want to. Once he asked my brother and me to watch as he, in taupe gabardine suit, shiny Italian shoes, and continental cologne walked by a certain well-dressed, bejeweled woman. She'll follow me with her eyes, he said. And she did.

My interest in black boys, and eventually men, was not political. The good-looking Irish-Catholic boys in my neighborhood didn't know what to do with me. They liked me, they were my friends, but because they saw me as smart, they never ever saw me as cute or sexy or kissable. It was a matter of respect, I guess, and because they respected me (a regard uncomfortably similar to what they felt for their mothers), well, slow dancing just wasn't likely. It had something to do with confession, conflicts of interest, catechism. I felt invisible around the good-looking Irish Catholic boys who fumbled with their mixed up, asensual ideas of girls with brains.

The black boys I knew did not seem confused by my tendency to want to be taken seriously, taken equally, or taken at all. They loved to slow dance, with me, without ambivalence. After withholding a natural outspokenness and the full expression of my libido with the boys on my suburban block, I had at last felt at home. When I danced in the dark with my friends from the Franklin Park Project, I did not feel as though I might be abetting a boy's fall from ecumenical grace; and when I had opinions or was passionate I did not feel as though I had committed a violation of my gender. Most of the black boys I knew were being raised by their single mothers, so they were not alarmed or discomforted by the many expressions of female vigor.

I went to the apartment of the man who played guitar twenty minutes after he invited me, and less than ten minutes after my mother warned me not to. I had decided it was time. At a gathering at our apartment the night before, my visiting brother and some friends had ragged me about being the only virgin in the room, and jokingly I had hinted at an imminent change in status. My mother, who had by this time abdicated her parental authority, sat quietly in the corner. I took her silence as disinterested consent. So the next day, within three hours of having caught his eye in the park, I found myself in his studio apartment amid boxes still unpacked and stacked halfway to the ceiling. I sat, docile, on his narrow, hard bed, waiting, while he played his guitar and sang, "Are you ready, to learn, to fall in lo-o-ove."

The music stopped, and in the dark orange of an early summer night, my shorts were at my ankles and he was pushing me into womanhood. I hurt and held my breath. He sweated and was surprised. I rolled over, stood up between the boxes, and reached for my shorts. He offered me a drink, but I said I'd be going. He asked if I wanted company, I declined, perfunctorily explored the evidence of my passage, closed my zipper, and walked home slowly and somewhat pleased, not knowing or caring whether I'd see him again. When I reached the apartment, I sat down on the couch, carefully, and my mother knew.

This man who became a boyfriend was no throbbing swoon of a teenage steady, whose class ring I flaunted and steamy car I secretly crept out of. He was dense with mystery, without family or steady friends, and held temporary jobs of which I was only vaguely aware. He was a place to get lost and be held. My friends barely knew about him. I knew if they did they'd warn me, and I didn't want to hear it. For a year I fell into his bed, and found enough comfort next to his flesh to forget about the family I had just lost.

I couldn't say where he came from or why, really, he wanted to be with me. Because he was the One who had taken me to sex, he probably didn't want to leave me there and liked that I wanted to know more. He may have felt a kind of custodial affection for this girl whom he viewed as his deflowered charge.

That summer, after my mother had left, with no place else

to go and because they would always have me, I decided to move in with my grandparents and my brother, into their warm, hokey, clean four-bedroom house in Benton. Within a few weeks I found myself missing my boyfriend's smell, his thick arms. It was then that I took the bus to Boston to be with him and became pregnant.

8

My grandmother's house was the sunny, doily-filled, un-changing set of a fifties sitcom where nothing, you'd ever believe, could get any more serious than a bad frost or a canceled choir practice. Altie's cabinets were full of food, and her warm rooms were cushioned by the safe comfort of small order everywhere—crocheted napkin holders and laminated place mats, cloth calendars (most outdated by years) painted with seasonal still lifes of harvested corn and pumpkins or holly-bordered Christmas bells; a chipped ceramic Boston terrier gazed longingly out a window, and a decorative cuckoo clock, whose bird sat stiff in the dark and never sang, tilted on a wall. Altie ironed underwear and scrubbed her kitchen sink until it gleamed. Her home was a pocket of dull, warm contentment kept happily clean and harmless, a perfect environmental antidote to cramped, unauthorized apartment living.

But the Benton of my childhood had faded by now. Over the years my friends in Boston had become more important than my grandmother or comic books. My grandmother's town was still a small, sweet-smelling community in the mid-dle of New Hampshire (the population had stayed at four hundred for over a hundred years), and it was almost entirely unfazed by the social and political tensions the sixties seemed to agitate. Grange assemblies, the Rainbow Girls, and Tuesday night firehouse meetings were the only places where groups of people met to change something, and usually it was just the calendar or the kinds of pies to be served at the Town Hall Saturday night turkey supper.

Benton was outside the action where I wanted to be. It began to matter to me that the chief of police was a hippie-hating vigilante, and that I saw my grandmother as simpleminded, getting hopelessly older, and the cause of everything my mother had grown to hate.

By the time I arrived as a displaced sixteen-year-old, I had already begun to see Benton as the viciously mundane locale of my mother's turn for the worse. Weatherworn farmers, aproned housewives, and dirty kids spent whole days in a state of Preparation (for cold weather, hard times, a heat wave, a summer garden, or death). To enjoy the moment and not fear the next was an indication of being lazy, or having time on your hands (and all the axioms about idleness firmly applied in Benton). Making do was as good as it got. To want more was treason.

I started to see my grandmother's steadiness as a liability to my teenage individuation. She became a failed, last-ditch replacement for the mother I had lost. My grandmother's strongest words in praise were "He's always just the same," meaning his temperament, expression, and thoughts were predictable and likely never to leap out of middle ground. When my grandmother disapproved of a woman, she could be heard murmuring under her breath, "Well, y'know she reads them novels," meaning that this woman dared to possess interests beyond the daily sort; that this life, in general, and that she and Benton, in particular, were not enough to hold a person's ear or thoughts. She took a woman's taste for fiction personally. Besides, novels tended to toy with the imagination and were littered with divorcées. My mother read novels, starting at the age of six. Nana, who had always taken pride in Sara's academic success, regarded her daughter's appetite for all books with prideful exception.

In my grandmother's town, nearly everyone suspected outsiders, and outsiders were everyone except an immutable core of multigenerational residents whose only travel out of town was generally sponsored by the military or provoked by medical emergencies. I was an outsider, schooled in Boston, offspring of a native who had defected and returned only in summer, when the roads were clear and the air was warm, when it was easy to live on the plains at the foot of the Ridge. But being the granddaughter of Altie H. Smith, grande dame of natives, didn't hurt. I always knew that.

Altie's roots went way back. She was one of three girls in a family of eleven kids and dozens of cousins, most of whom were born and died in Benton. Altie's sister Ethel happily and often exited the daughterly milieu of the family kitchen for the stables—her passion was horses—leaving the breadmaking and dress hemming to her younger sister. Altie, aproned from the age of thirteen (probably as much for the comfort on her big body as for its usefulness), did her filial duties plus Ethel's undone share.

My grandmother took care of her brothers and Ethel until they died; and when she was seventeen, Altie Hayes nursed her ailing sister Margaret, with whom she shared a bedroom until Margaret's early death from the influenza of 1918 at the age of nine. My grandmother would recall, always with tears, how on the day of her beloved sister's funeral large black horses whose heads bobbed above fifteen-foot snowdrifts hauled a child-size casket in a dark carriage to the cemetery through a blaze of snow, away from the house for the last time.

My brother was my grandmother's perfect boy. Nana always had at least three or four prints of his yearbook photo displayed in her house, at least one of them hanging on the wall next to but slightly higher than her collection of Jesus Christ icons. This same photo, of a bang-swept, big-eyed, self-possessed young man, appeared in the *Devon Courier* on several occasions to accompany reports of what his grandmother considered newsworthy accomplishments. When he made the dean's list, when he started his work-study job, or when he returned to his grandmother's house for the summer to work, the Benton correspondent (my grandmother's sister-in-law Bessie) received a gloating press release, in longhand, way before deadline, with "photo enclosed." One summer my grandmother took over the column. She was shameless.

I was Nana's only other grandchild. We sewed, were sentimental gossipers, and shopped. We'd go "down the line" (to the next town over) and travel the squeaky wooden floors of Woolworth's as privileged navigators on a luxury cruise. We inched down aisles jammed with gaudy ashtrays and brilliant, fake adjustable rings, surrounded by the heavy smells of rubber dolls and malted milk balls and spearmint jellies piled high in glass cases at the front of the store. As I got older we talked births and deaths, food and childhood, and I know she loved being with me. But for my grandmother, my presence was not the honor of male company.

She was convinced that boys, and all males were boys, depended on women to determine what they would eat and when and other life-preserving basics. My grandfather gave in early to Altie's willfulness, and often asked his wife whether it was sweater weather or if he should wear his rubbers. I remember him sitting at the kitchen table, like an impatient preschooler at snack time, waiting to see what treat my grandmother had deemed sensible and would be willing to serve.

My brother would have none of her overzealous nurturing, especially as he got older, but his committed resistance to it simply tickled her and inflated her already adorable idea of him as a man of his own. She grew more devoted to her grandson by the day because of the depth of his responsible devotion to her. He took very thorough, committed care of his grandmother—he fixed stairs, fought on her behalf with plumbers who charged an old woman too much, and noticed a new dress. "Bless his heart," she'd say when he'd spent the morning shoveling her out after a winter storm. Her daughter's son was, as a result, one of two men in the universe upon whom Altie Smith could and would depend. (The Son of God was the other.)

The joy she got from her grandson seemed to heal in an instant all the trials in her daily life—her daughter's hostility, the deaths of friends, her husband's racking emphysema. She seemed to twirl, giddy and as light-footed as a corpulent woman could be, when finally he came in through the kitchen to the smell of her pies, home at last.

As my mother aged, the disagreements between her and her mother intensified. My mother railed against my grandmother for feeding my brother and me too much; our Nana was purposefully fattening her grandchildren, because, in my mother's mind, she had become the conniving witch in the forest of the abandoned Hansel and Gretel. If we were fat, nobody would love us except her, and she would have us all to herself. As I grew older, less the enamored granddaughter and more the protective daughter, I sympathized with my mother and reacted by quickly faulting my grandmother, bloating her errors to ugly proportions too. I felt my mother's hurt and rage, joined the cause, and never questioned her target.

Though I cannot know the intricacies of their mother-daughter tie, looking back I can see how my grandmother could have overlooked a child's search for self. It was not Altie's nature to decipher a small girl's hunger for comfort in an alien world. This would have been a subtlety she would've missed. My grandmother's indelicate, yet sympathetic, approach to the lives of her loved ones inhibited her ability to spot trouble of the complex kind.

Death, illness, birth, and obvious disasters were her specialities; she confronted the unalloyed need and met it. Altie picked up hitchhikers, nursed the dying, and fed the poor. Subsequently, many of her young daughter's emotional needs went undetected, such as when Sara begged her mother to stay home one Saturday because she didn't want to be alone. My mother remembers feeling the chilly breeze of her mother's big coat in her face as Altie hurried past her toward the door. She promised to buy Sara something special on the way home, then left.

But my grandmother's steadiness served as an effective foil for a child's anguish. Altie was both constant and resilient. My mother felt her childhood was an injustice; that she was given away so long after her birth (after her mother must have known the baby she was leaving) and acquired by a family so dissimilar, in a place so foreign to her natural sensibility, were circumstances that begged for blaming. But the person (her natural mother) and the circumstances that had put her there were either absent or unknown, and out of earshot. My grandmother was there to buffer her anger, and my grandmother would always be there.

If long-gone mothers become imagined heroes, then the mothers who stay forgo, while alive, their children's poetic memorials and pay the price of mortal imperfection and, often, the debt of other disappearing adults.

My grandmother slayed phantom deserters with single-minded exuberance, stepping over their rotting carcasses, a hero to future children whose mothers dared leave. But self-conscious heroics were not what drove her. She possessed the faith of the ingenuous. She was unafraid of her first impulse.

I will never forget when my brother returned from school one day, announcing his suspension for having long hair, and how my sixty-eight-year-old grandmother huffed with indignation, filled her kitchen with outrage, flung her flour-dusted apron onto a chair, and headed, in her crisscross canvas house shoes, to the school of the misguided principal seventeen miles away.

"Did you ever think," she fumed, eye to eye with the crew-cut principal, "that he might not like *your* hair?" My brother was promptly reinstated.

Scenes like that convey vivid, lasting messages to the harbored. My grandmother was the Protector, the kind children dream about, the flying, all-powerful variety. She made things move, ran interference. She had nothing to lose that mattered; her family mattered most. Though she did not appear to understand her daughter and her daughter's relatives, all she seemed to need to know was that we belonged to her; that was enough.

My grandmother's sense of loyalty was her best lesson. But for years I could not see this. When my mother grew sick and I entered my adolescence, my grandmother became the enemy; for me she did not exist outside her guilty part in raising a child who had become a suffering woman, my mother. Not long ago I realized that if I wanted to understand my history I would have to stop seeing the women before me for their part in each other's lives and begin to see them for their place in mine, unencumbered by childhood loyalties.

53

Now, long after she has died, and after her daughter, my mother, has disappeared, I see a different woman; Altie's essence is so perceptible, her spirit, too late, so plain. Without her forbearance during my pregnancy, I would've fallen into an isolation so deep that, I am sure, reemergence would've taken more years than I could sanely spare.

9

My grandmother was the first one to notice I was pregnant. She knew it before I did (or before I was willing to admit it).

"Janny," she said, heaving her broad, corseted body onto the edge of my bed as I stifled a nagging cough. "You don't have to say so, but you haven't menstruated for a while, have you?" I hadn't, but who was counting? I knew I wasn't eating much, but I was gaining weight and had suddenly found tuna fish and onions repugnant. I stood, from time to time, in front of the bathroom mirror and saw, even after I had sucked in my stomach as far as it would go, a threatening paunch. Okay. So I was gaining muscle. Stomach muscle.

I was masterminding a pathetic scheme, an onrushing crisis made less stoppable by the day. If I had kept track of my periods and if I hadn't played with the proof, my stomach would not have grown into an emergency begging for help. I would've had the time to make a choice. Instead, I chose a slow sleeper of a tantrum that guaranteed nobody's reasonable intervention until it was too late. My pregnancy, as hoped for on some very desperate level, would be completed.

Ignored pregnancies, the conceptions that are defaulted into existence, are often mistaken for mistakes. If we females know anything, we know what our bodies can do. We feel it—our visceral inheritance—hoard it like a rich aunt's gems, and cash it in when we are desperate or ready to wear rubies. Even without the biology, we have the instincts to tell us where our power lies, and we know how to get to it.

Education is not the answer to so-called unplanned or teenage pregnancy: The solution is another kind of lesson, which begins at birth, one that will teach a girl to take charge of her sorrow or anger and not use her body against herself when she thinks it is the only authority she has. We starve, sell, bloat, and impregnate our bodies. We back away from unladylike rage and turn inward to do our damage, dumping our anger or despair within. I was not contraceptively igno-rant. I had birth control pills I decided not to take. I was a frantic girl, using what sparse language I had to call for my mother.

My brother and I, as urban intruders, pulled together as seniors on the fringe at Heywood Regional High School. We took the bus to our high school, waiting every morning at the post office with other Benton kids whom we barely knew. One morning, just as my brother and I arrived at the bus stop, a sudden hot wave enveloped me. My legs gave out as I accordioned down to the cold curb. My brother asked if I was all right, but I couldn't even grunt or part my lips to answer. My head had flopped onto the tops of my knees, and my boneless arms dangled by my sides. With what little con-sciousness I had, I heard the quick slap of my brother's sneak-ers race in the direction of our grandmother's house. I was barely aware of how awkward I must've looked, but I could not rearrange my limbs or lift my head, and I lost hearing every few seconds. I went in and out of darkness waiting for my brother to come back.

It was nothing serious, only the flu (accompanied perhaps by a nasty accumulation of suppressed morning sickness). But if I hadn't been out of school, at home sick for a week, I wonder how long it would have taken me, or anyone, to come right out and say it, to state the obvious.

When the flu wouldn't leave, Dr. Atkinson was called to my bedside. "Could I see you in my office tomorrow," he said, "by yourself?"

The next day was bitter cold, so my grandmother heated up her car before I emerged from the house in layers of clothes on my first trip out in days. We rode in silence to Dr. Atkinson's office, which was in a small white house across from the Elton Cemetery, where gravestones leaned into Veteran's Day flags that snapped in a mean breeze, and thin, brown geraniums, leftover from Sundays, huddled together on balding grass.

In his office the doctor got to the point. "There is a swelling in your abdomen," he said. "I want to have a look." He asked me to undress. I slowly shed the tiers of my winter clothing and climbed onto the table. He pressed in the sides of my stomach and kneaded my abdomen. In less than a minute he asked me to sit up and get dressed. He turned on his heel, grabbed his elbows, and kept his eyes on the floor.

"You are pregnant," he said, unhappily. There. Someone had said it. The calculated, obvious fact of my pregnancy had been announced. I asked, pleading through tears, about an abortion. But abortion was never part of the plan, really. If my pregnancy could've been terminated then, within that week, I would've still been a motherless daughter, without a crisis, a mere student in a stupid school, an outsider in my town. With this news, I was at the center of my own drama, and changes would have to come.

No, he said, not at five months you don't. I lifted my backside off the sticky table, wiped my eyes, clenched my mouth shut to stop the rising sobs, and fixed myself to face my grandmother. But this disaster was not meant for her.

I told her without looking up on our way out of the office. She sighed, "Oh, Janny," and we walked to the car.

In 1969 I had only heard of but never known anyone who had had an abortion. I had heard about expensive, clandestine trips to New York, about uncertain recoveries. I knew no details until a few months later, when my friend Estelle★ tried to end her mistaken pregnancy. When she was two months pregnant, she visited a man with dirty hands in a dark walk-up under the noisy trains at Dudley Station in Boston, who, for $175, gave her an illegal bottle of pills, which she was told would end her pregnancy. Estelle took the pills, and for the next two days her body expelled tissue and massive amounts of blood. Two months later, without having had a period, Estelle made an appointment with a doctor who told her she was four months pregnant. Her pregnancy had not ended; the pills had not worked. Estelle lived every minute of the re-maining months of her pregnancy sure she would have a wasted, incomplete, or dead infant. But in her ninth month she barely got to the hospital in time to push out a healthy eight-pound girl, whose beginning will always haunt her.

I had no choices left. My body was veering irreversibly in the wrong direction. The teenage-woman body I had barely begun to live in was leaving as quickly as it had arrived. I had just started to like how my waist arched in above my blue-jeaned behind when my stomach began pulling my jeans in the other direction. My newly formed hips, menstruating womb, and still-forming breasts were barely prepared for the full-blown work of reproduction, and for the tugging, push-ing, and feeding of a smaller body inside.

Seventeen and ambivalently pregnant, I felt like a child newly awakened from a nap—disoriented and passive, walk-ing from one day to the next in an agitated trance, waiting to be fully alert, looking for a lap. For the next three and a half months I felt first like the reluctant host to a persistent lodger; then I merged with this baby against a world that had turned rotten. We would be covictims, conspirators in a subplot to call up my missing mother (though I didn't know that then). This baby would be my appended, carry-on company, the cure to my vacant self I had howled for months before.

A month after I found out I was pregnant, my mother called from San Francisco, where she had fled with the divorce money and was being, for the first time since her early teens, an unmarried woman and a childless mother. When I told her I was pregnant, she was furious. Even amid the unreliable addresses and poverty of our family's postdivorce chaos, and at the heart of her mental illness, my mother had been deliberate about getting her daughter contraception. When I lost my virginity, I told her, and the next day I was sitting in the office of a gynecologist looking at small yellow pills in aluminum packets. So when she called from the road, she was not prepared for the news of her daughter's pregnancy. She thought she had at the least headed off that disaster.

She hadn't known that instead, two weeks after she had moved out of our apartment, I had moved out too, and left packages containing two months' worth of birth control pills standing upright in the rusted corner cabinet of our galley kitchen. I knew exactly where they were when I grabbed the broom and checked the lights before I walked out of our apartment for the last time. If my mother was going to walk, I, for one, was not about to collude with her easy exit. I stared down those pills menacingly, as if they were my mother's stand-in—a resented, lousy baby-sitter. I saw contraception as part of her escape plan, a package of prevention in her absence, to avert a catastrophe that might interrupt her flight from family, and I was damned if would go along. I would *not* be the levelheaded girl she counted on me to be. She was not being even a little of what I had hoped she would be—there, for starters. In a macabre collision of fears—my mother's run from another rejection and my reaction to her rejection of me—another child's birth into abandonment was about to be guaranteed.

On the phone from the West Coast, she said she would come back. And that was all I heard.

I waited for my mother's arrival before I went back to Heywood to officially drop out. I told no one why I was leaving, not even my art teacher, Daniel Farrell,* who, along with his family, had provided refuge and friendship to my brother and me during our year at Heywood High School. But as I left the school parking lot for the final time, he approached the car.

"You know," he said, bringing his head down to meet my eyes, "I don't want you to feel any pressure about this, but we've been trying to adopt a baby." And then he told me that people at adoption agencies had been giving him and his wife, Linette, a hard time about his meager salary and his family's lack of religion. It had been a disappointing fiasco, he said; they were about to give up, and oh, they had hoped for an ethnic child. I didn't know he knew. The sound of his request, so specific (one brown child, to go), unnerved me, and I felt mildly protective of the child within me, who it seemed was being claimed by an interested customer. I cannot remember saying anything, though I probably did say something polite, but at that moment, in my sixth month, I thought about adoption for the first time.

10

Having been called back to her family by her daughter's dilemma, my mother returned, albeit unfinished and still hungry, from her initiation, at thirty-four, as an unencumbered woman. All would not be lost, though. She would be around for my third and final trimester of pregnancy and, of course, for the birth of her first grandchild. But she had been yanked, it became clear, from a preferred place.

Nana, my brother, and I endured my mother's vicious mood swings for about a month after her return. Then she was gone again, brought against her will to a hospital in a depressingly regrettable crisis of faith. Her meanness had peaked; she had physically threatened my grandmother and spewed angry delusions at my brother and me, whom she still blamed for conspiring against her. We were spying on her. Her wasted, isolated childhood was the fault of my grandmother. The System had made me pregnant. We tried taming or soothing her in every way we knew; we were firm, understanding, logical, sometimes loving and sad. I would sit on the edge of my chair in the living room across from her, stiff with determination, raw and afraid, look into her face and reject her delusions, word for word. Couldn't she see that I loved her? Didn't she know me enough to know that I would never do such a thing? She would counter with more accusations, and I would become silent and disoriented, until the next bout of optimism. We agreed with her, we explained ourselves, we pleaded reality.

My grandmother would end up saying she was sorry, on the verge of tears, her face brutalized by sadness, with her hands buried in the twisted knots of her apron, even though she could not understand why she should be sorry. My grandmother never blamed her deluded daughter; and, as frightened as she became when my mother threw things and screamed, she never fought back, because she didn't know how to turn against her own child. My brother and I were righteously indignant, though I hung my head more often than he, and he fought her tirades more vigorously than I.

Finally we were defeated by hopelessness and called for help, a last resort; the Benton chief of police came, and we forced my mother from our house into an institution.

For the remaining two months of my pregnancy, my brother and I visited our mother every Sunday in confinement. (She did not want to see Nana.) We would find her subdued, teary and alone, in someone else's oversized polyester clothes, hunched over in a metal chair against a paint-chipped wall, pushing yarn through plastic cards, drowning in a roomful of patients' deep-throated protests and the stale aroma of instant potatoes and smoke. At the exact minute our mother saw us, she would begin to cry, as if she had been waiting to break and was too embarrassed to give in while alone. I remember the agony of having to hold back—from holding her, from shedding tears of my own, from gushing with apology, from trying again to make sense. I sat with my coat pulled tightly across my stomach to cover the pregnancy that had caused her such disappointment, while my brother asked responsible questions, which in the end were pointless. Nothing was being done to help my mother. The psychiatrist had seen her twice in six weeks, and she was being sedated and ignored. She pleaded with us to take her home, but it wasn't advised, and we didn't know how or if we should. So every Sunday my brother and I got into my grandmother's Chevrolet without our mother and made the trip back home in silence. We told our grandmother she was doing fine.

After I left school in my senior year, I spent weeks at a time in Boston with my boyfriend, who was "crashing" at a different buddy's place each time I visited. I spent entire days awkwardly alone in the spare rooms of strangers' apartments, sustained by potato soup and the occasional crispy glazed donut from the bakery thrift shop on the corner. And I waited, sometimes days, for my boyfriend to return from places he never talked about. He seemed disinterested in my health, this pregnancy, the eventual baby.

Back in Benton, I watched TV or lay under the covers in the company of my cat in a tiny back bedroom with a low, slanted ceiling and a small window, in between thoughtlessness and sleep. My grandmother tried to feed me. Occasionally I considered ways to hide my stomach.

I had a dress, a stiff, boxy orange shift my mother had made, which did not give in to the ovate curve of my front, and I wore it on public outings. That, with a coat or puffy sweater draped over my forearms clasped together in front of the crucial spot, served as a subtle foil. It was the dress I wore when I went to my high school to drop out, and when I went to a concert for which I had bought tickets long in advance, with friends who had no idea of my pregnancy, and who, long after, never knew.

I went to the store in my grandfather's oversized wool jacket, hid upstairs when my brother's friends came over, walked into the bathroom if I knew a neighbor was about to stop by, and sat in silence on the commode for as long as the visit took. I did not discuss my pregnancy on the phone with best friends. A classmate stopped hearing from me when I left school, but if I saw her by chance at the general store, I would stand angled away from her near the door, without mention of my swollen stomach, expecting her conspiratorial oblivion and a hurried exchange. Then I would step quickly out of her sight.

My brother stayed close, making up, it seemed, for the absence of others, and watched carefully over a sister who had taken a terribly wrong turn. I was marooned in limbo, never knowing whether to be annoyed by the lump that had grown into the front of my body or to become one with the blooming life inside. What I ought to be doing, I thought, was hidden in the silences of those around me, and I could find the answers if I looked or listened hard enough. My grandmother, I always sensed, was holding back tides of want. I knew how she loved babies, but she never said what she expected me to do, only that I had her with me whatever my decision. "You do," she'd say, "jeshew you want."

For as long as I had known her, my grandmother had had a longing for babies, which she tempered by sewing doll clothes and overfeeding Boston terriers and birds. One morning we woke to a canary lying stiff on its back, its feet pointed skyward, as if surrendering to its impossibly vast menu. She had always had an unwieldy yet unfulfilled desire to nurture, to have children and to grow them. But because a doctor had failed to diagnose, or believe in time, Altie's complaints about severe menstrual discomfort, she was unable to have children of her own.

When she made the trip to the hospital, believing that the tumors that had finally been found and that had kept her from conceiving would be taken away at last, she was relieved, eager to try again to make the babies she had waited so long for. She told me, "'Course we came home and thought that was it. Now we'd have children." But after many months of trying, she went back to her doctor. He laughed at her. Of course you're not pregnant, he said, you've had a hysterectomy. She would tell this story laughing, too.

Once, during the seventh month of my pregnancy, I gave in, self-consciously, defiantly, to a maternal urge. My grandmother and I were shopping, and I had decided to buy yarn, two fluffy, baby-colored skeins of yarn; I was caught up in our euphoric shopping bond, and caved in to a blend of our secret wishes. I bought a pattern for baby booties, and I would dare to knit this baby something for its minuscule feet. The appearance of yarn would help to diffuse the cloying sadness in our house or at least help to stir up a response.

I returned from the store with my grandmother, who thought the yarn was pretty, jumped out of the car, and announced to my brother, who was parking a bike, my intention to knit. He looked at me and shook his head.

"No," he said, pained. "No, Jan."

I shrank back into the seat. I did not know, and was afraid to decide, my plan for this baby. So estranged was I from my own instincts that I deferred to anyone with an opinion— especially my brother. I had imbued him with the veto power of an A-bomb. In the absence of parents I had crowned him the overseer; I was hungry for the guidance he was willing to give. So when my brother, my guardian, my pal, my family, revealed his stinging solution, I crawled back into the car, stuffed the corny yarn under my fat, stretching stomach, and sat in silence until I could swallow a twisting ache stuck in my throat.

★   ★   ★

That is how I remembered it. Since then, I have spoken with my brother about this, and he remembered it differently. He said when he saw the yarn, it was the first indication he had that I was pregnant. I thought he knew—that my grandmother or I had told him after returning from the doctor's office. But no one had. My grandmother, I realize now, considered the news mine to disclose. And after hearing the formal diagnosis, I must've boarded up my insides, leaving even my brother, so important to me, locked out. My brother had been left outside of what he respectfully calls "the world of women"—the circulation of information exclusive to the lives of females *among* females—and saw the yarn, simply, as my tentative clue of embarrassing, bad news, not, as I thought, of my intention to keep my baby.

"My reaction came to your announcement that you were pregnant, not to any decision about keeping the baby," he said, years later. "I *was* unhappy about the pregnancy. I felt true regret, given your ambitious dreams." My brother and I traded pauses and pondered together but separately the long-gone significance of our twenty-four-year misunderstanding.

11

Nineteen sixty-nine was the year of the Woodstock Music Festival, and I didn't even know it. I was busy. For years after the sixties milestone I'd hear stories about sleeping in fields, drugs, nakedness, the transcendental belonging. And for years I felt as though grand larceny had been committed against my youth. I felt robbed.

Smug prophets on dope questioned authority and were taken seriously enough to make the evening news, which I watched with envy and from far away; not being your parents (suspect for their dispirited acceptance of all things established), or anyone at all over thirty, was reason enough to rejoice. Members of the postwar population swell had the numbers, the sway, the stage to make a difference. Girlfriends went to "Women's Liberation" meetings in the dark basements of Unitarian churches, sipped tea, and felt furtively avant-garde, readying for the revolution. It was after the Pill and before AIDS. It was definitely a time to be young and female.

What I remember most about 1969 is May 19, and what I'll never forget about that day is the shallow breaths and the wet, warm weight of a baby on my emptied womb. The flesh-and-heat arrival of my infant girl redeemed, for a moment, the crazy pain of the previous six hours and made quick sense of the misery of the months before.

Early in the morning on May 18, I had awakened with pelvic flutters. Because I knew so little, actually nothing, about what labor pains should feel like, I figured this was it. I stepped deliberately downstairs into the coffee-strong kitchen, cradling my mysteriously twitching abdomen in my hands, as if readjusting it would alter the tugging inside.

My grandmother was at the table eating toast when I walked toward her, fighting contractions. I said nothing. She must've seen something in my face, because she lifted her body out of her chair, put her cup in the sink, and walked to the closet to get her coat.

My prenatal education was meager. I vaguely remember my few visits with Dr. Bradford, who, because he seemed to be certain that this baby would be given up or taken away and that I had been foolish to begin with, canceled appointments more than once and appeared to take little interest in my health or the development of the fetus.

Dr. Bradford was a short, rectangular mass of a man whose hair peaked in pure white tufts at the top sides of his wide head. He spoke in brief, gruff sentences, sharing what little information he had with his shoes, and seemed to aim for the image of a rural, Rockwellian physician, falling pathetically short. He would attempt chummy and come off cloying. He tried to be funny and was not. He didn't seem to want to touch me. His paternalistic distance left me more mystified and worried after each visit, and it took me hours after I left his office to feel free from stirrups.

He listened to the fetal heartbeat only twice (and never shared it with me), and was uninterested in my weight, diet, smoking habit, heredity factors, and blood pressure. He never let me in on the information he had about my body, this baby. My prenatal care, which began only in my sixth month of pregnancy, consisted wholly of the daily challenge of swallowing fuchsia vitamins the size of stones.

I chain-smoked in the car as my grandmother followed the road steadily to Franklin Memorial Hospital, where I had been born seventeen years earlier. I was as scared as I could be, while being as numb as I had ever been.

My grandmother was with me for most of the day. My brother came soon after I arrived. When they left, I walked the halls, wincing, fighting the quick pull of cramps every ten minutes, then every five minutes until I was brought to a bed in the labor room, where I watched black-and-white TV until contractions began to defeat me. Just about the time *The Smothers Brothers Comedy Hour* came on, 9:00 P.M. on Sunday, I began to rock and shriek, bewildered, shredding my hospital-issue nightgown and my sheets. Stunned by a strange agony, I writhed semiconsciously on the edges of my bed. My grandmother, who had never experienced childbirth, could not tell me what to expect. My mother, who had often gloated about the ease with which she had given birth, was not available. One nurse on her way off her shift poked her irritated face into my room and was inconvenienced by the mess and the noise I was trying not to make. I was trying to behave. The nurse lifted up the bars on the side of the bed, afraid I would tumble out, sucked her teeth, and left.

Nobody mentioned anything about blurting noises, pummeling one's bedding—and certainly nothing was ever said about breathing exercises. I felt foolishly weak-souled because I was out of control and had to fight an overwhelming impulse to whine, *very* loudly. (I grew up thinking that complaining was unfavorable at any age, under any circumstance.

In my family writing a letter to the editor or changing one's course was the preferred outlet for discontent. Under the extreme conditions of childbirth, however, neither resolution seemed within reach. So I tried to be as considerately undisruptive as a person in agony could be.) I spent the remaining three hours holding yelps inside my jaws and feeling as if I were squirming in deep scalding water without buoyancy.

I wish someone—anyone—would've said something like "This is normal. And your howling, we expected that too." I wish I had had a hand to grip.

Years later, I began talking with an old friend, Alice,* whom Dr. Bradford had also attended during her first delivery, a year after my baby was born. She too was unmarried, and she remembered something the doctor had told her in the final, agonizing minutes of her long labor. For unmarried mothers, he said bluntly, we try to make the labors as rough as possible, "so you girls will think twice before making a second mistake." And with that, he shot out of her room and intercepted a nurse on her way to Alice's bedside with ice and towels.

Up until about fifteen minutes before I gave birth, I suffered a six-hour solitude in an airless, lima bean green labor room, quarantined for stupidity, pleading for relief. Then one nurse was kind. She cooled me down and changed my tattered hospital gown. She said it wouldn't be long now.

I was given a caudal and wheeled into a cool, metal room, where, in the early-morning quiet, at 1:05 A.M., under a soft spotlight, masked people delivered a baby from me and placed her on my stomach. The doctor and several nurses talked softly, and then the baby disappeared. I didn't want her to go but didn't dare speak. I asked the gender of my baby three times before I was heard, then sobbed quietly when they told me she was a girl. I was wheeled into a room where three other mothers slept in the dark, and, in the small splash of a night-light, I lay awake, relieved, drunk with sorrow and shock.

The next day the disinterested doctor visited me, poked my deflated body, observed my engorged breasts, and helped me onto a scale. I wanted to see the baby. No, said the doctor without explanation, on his way out of the room. The decision, it appeared, had been made. But nobody had asked me.

Being married seemed to make the difference in New England twenty-five years ago. There had always been pregnant teenagers in Benton. In fact, postmarriage, planned pregnancy was rare in this town where college was unheard of, reproduction and marriage (usually in that order) was the chief plan for female adult life, and duty-bound males "did the right thing," often without love. My own mother, pregnant at sixteen, had had a well-attended white Benton wedding.

But I had no intention to marry. My only plan, unknown to me then, was that of an expectant daughter awaiting the arrival of a mother. Because my unconscious plot excluded the sponsorship of a husband, I remained the unpaired charge of the community, and the baby-to-be, it seemed, would be dealt with by committee.

Once, in my eighth month of pregnancy, one of many neighbors who stood by their windows and pushed their curtains to the side saw me ride by on a bike. She called my grandmother and reported that I was involved in risky activity for a mother-to-be and that Altie ought to summon me home pronto. My grandmother cited my very good health and declined to accept, thanks anyway, the neighbor's advice.

Because I was the unripe carrier who knew not what she had done, I had lost my place on the decision-making panel. Consequently, what to do with the Error, such as terminate it, give it away, or bring it up, became the agenda of less stupid, more responsible people, such as neighbors, doctors, older relatives, and married people everywhere. I was an ungrown female who did not have the strength to be a parent or the heart to be a mother.

After the doctor flatly refused to let me see my baby for the second time, I dared to walk to the nursery to see female, Waldron. When I finally spotted her among the babies on the third day, I stared for a few long, perilous seconds, unable to break my gaze. I could hardly make the connection. I saw a fully formed, coffee-colored baby with shiny black waves of hair, almond-shaped eyes, and perfect hands. That I, so slight of self and lost, could have grown and delivered such a perfect girl was barely believable. I had no idea where I fit into this unhappy mess.

One of the three women with whom I shared my room wanted to know why the doctor had withheld my baby. I told her I had kind of decided I would give her up, but then, after all I had been through, I wasn't so sure. One woman with dark hair stuffed into a multicolored scarf, who had just given birth at the age of forty-three to a sixth child, was near tears. She was convinced I should not go through with it.

"Don't do it," she said. "You'll regret it for as long as you live." The other women were listening, and soon there were three official, indignant mothers, voices of maternal experience and authority, making policy. Demand, they counseled, as members of a convincing committee, to see your baby.

I asked for my baby again. Again, the doctor said no, it wouldn't be good for me if I was giving her up. And I was giving her up, wasn't I? Well, I said timidly, I wasn't sure. What do you mean? he said, infuriated. He left the room before I could tell him.

I finally told my grandmother I wanted to hold my baby. She knew the doctor and made things move. I held the baby I named Simone when she was three days old. Her small, warm bulk in my arms felt like having my body back, the one I had left three days earlier. I was almost afraid to see her face, to look at her eyes. Simone, I thought, you are too beautiful for this ragged beginning.

After I held my baby, I lapsed into thoughts of motherhood. It showed. I wanted to hold her as often as possible. But nobody talked. My grandmother began to buy baby clothes; my brother worried speechlessly from the corners of the hospital room. My maternal roommates beamed approvingly when I held and fed Simone. And I began to have visitors.

My art teacher, Daniel Farrell, and his wife, Linette, were among them.

12

In the sixties, even when teachers could go floral and get away with it, the faculty at Heywood Regional High School stayed gray-suited and close-cropped. My brother was editor of the school literary magazine, and the faculty adviser nearly edited the publication bare every time, claiming insubordinate messages and activism between the lines. At Heywood, whose principal had tried unsuccessfully to eject my shaggy-haired brother, nobody was questioning authority.

My brother and I would eat lunch together, comrades amid the repression, and could be seen talking with each other in the hallways between classes. Such sibling harmony was suspect, so we were rumored to be lovers.

Daniel Farrell, a young family man and artist with reckless red hair who wore lopsided vests, baggy pants, and sneakers, taught me how to paint with egg tempera, the history behind Picasso's *Guernica,* and how to survive humorless teachers. The principal and faculty thought he was odd, clearly not one of their own, and failed to renew his contract after one year. But for the few months I was there, the irreverent Mr. Farrell provided what little humor and comfort I was to experience at school that year. Out of school, my brother and I found in him and his family's company a warm retreat from our isolated life with old grandparents, and as urban transplants in hostile territory.

When we came to dinner at their worn-down wooden farmhouse, Daniel would provide predinner wit and inspirational counsel (like what colleges to apply to) while Linette, whom he had met at art college, would serenely prepare food as her two young children raced giggling into her skirt; she seemed to have a high tolerance for disorder.

Linette Farrell was a slight woman, whose long, black hair waved in close to her small face and around dark eyes. She had small, capable hands that worked the kitchen, designed complicated home-sewn costumes for her children, and painted landscapes in oil. The certainty of her devotion to her husband was daunting, and she poured love and trust into her children without hesitation.

Daniel beamed with proud pleasure around his wife. He seemed to be both in awe of her creative grace and smug about his good sense at having chosen such a wonder. They were at home with each other, bound by an understanding to live well no matter how little money there was, and there was often none. Customarily, the Farrells fought off the wolf at the door with the coincidental, usually minor sale of art, kept their car afloat by trading with neighbors who knew about engines, and ate all year from a generous summer garden. Their house always smelled good and was filled with oil paintings, pencil sketches, and a bathtub full of turtles, whose lives Daniel observed up close and whom he loved to render in earth-toned watercolors.

When Dr. Atkinson had confirmed my pregnancy during Christmas break from school, my immediate plan was to become housebound. Being seen pregnant was not going to happen. Besides my visits to my mother, I rarely emerged from my grandmother's house, so I did not see the Farrells again until they visited me in the hospital the day after I had given birth to my daughter. Linette brought me a plant and asked how I was feeling. She was a welcome, soothing presence, because she seemed to be the only one who believed I was capable of keeping the baby I had just had. No one had even hinted at that idea. I told her I still didn't know what to do and said the words I thought I ought to: that being a mother was a big responsibility. Linette said responsibility was not a bad thing, and, really, what else was there? She didn't say much, but after she left I was sure I would keep this baby.

I had named my baby Simone, after Nina Simone, whom my mother, brother, and I—in a rare family outing—had seen in a nighttime concert near the beach two summers before and whose rich, lean voice had finally made sense of jazz for me. It was a sudden association.

My grandmother had prepared for the day I would arrive home with Simone—she had collected pastel knits, cotton diapers, and a secondhand white wicker bassinet on wheels. When my baby was handed to me on my way out of the hospital, I was both dazed and unbearably proud. But I did not get close to her.

When I got home, I was tired and sore. The baby's father, who had gratuitously imagined the son he would have, visited and held his daughter. He thought she was biracially beautiful—the idea appealed. But when he returned to Boston, he called, and I told him I didn't want to see him anymore. I still wasn't sure what I would do, but I was certain he had nothing to do with it. It was as if the crisis had come and gone, and I was beginning to hide the evidence, soberly sweeping up.

I was already drawing lines between past and present, and he was part of a history I wanted to bury.

Two days after my return from the hospital, I wore a slimming lime green minishift and sea green blouse, dressed my brown baby in deep yellows, and visited my mother in confinement. She wanted to come home, but she was not ready, the doctors said again. She wanted to help with the baby, we could do it together, she promised. Within a week, counting on her transcendent motherly and grandmotherly obligations to keep her on course, my mother was sprung from the hospital with a tiny yellow envelope of Thorazine, which would ensure her even temperament and lifeless smiles.

My mother had plotted her release, and I held the frail promise of her part in my life. We three generations had a single afternoon in the sun, Simone squiggling between us on a blanket on the flat, soft grass in the front yard of my grandmother's house. The next day my mother left for Boston to look for places for us to live, she said.

Simone would cry. My grandmother would pick her up, and I would become edgy because, I said, she shouldn't spoil her. It doesn't hurt to love 'em, she'd say. After about a week I withdrew, surrendering what little strength I had, and gave my baby over completely to the care of my grandmother.

In the mornings, Nana would cradle Simone in her wide hands as she squeezed spongefuls of soapy water over her small body. How she loves the water, my grandmother would call over her shoulder to me from the kitchen sink, as I sat dazed in front of a game show. The longer my mother stayed away, the more I became annoyed by my grandmother's joy. I pretended not to hear when she talked about this baby.

And then she'd clean her great-granddaughter's ears with

cotton, oil her hair, and pat her tiny limbs dry. After she powdered, diapered, and dressed the baby, she rocked and sang to her.

My grandmother, unaccustomed as she was to people of color, never saw Simone's so-called illegitimacy or brownness as an awkward liability in her small town. When a neighbor dared to ask, What'll people say? my grandmother shot back, "What in the ole Harry do I care what anybody thinks?"

My grandmother slept, in between my emphysemic grandfather's proclamations of life-ending last breaths, next to the bassinet on the first floor. During the night when the baby cried, she would pull her heavy, old body out of bed to feed and hold her in the dark. I slept upstairs and heard nothing.

My grandfather sat wordlessly during these weeks, on the outskirts of my grandmother's bustling delight. Occasionally, when only I was home, he would wince and suggest, barely audibly, that the baby was hungry or wet or needed burping. I ignored him.

I sulked, estranged in my grandparents' house, at odds with baby noises, irritable, and uncertain about what, if anything, mattered. I was marking time, exhausted by a begrudging detachment from everyone, everything—waiting for the worst to pass. Only it never did. It became hard and bitter work to stay emotionally suspended, and I wanted out.

One Sunday afternoon while my grandmother was at church, Simone began to howl. She was hungry, and I was mad. And at that moment, I knew what I must do. I knew that mad was what I should not be if I were truly a mother, if she were truly my daughter. Just as I suspected, just as I had been told, the reason I should release her to better parents presented itself. I was unfit, and here, on this Sunday afternoon, was the proof.

My mother called later that day.

"There's nothing we can do for her," she sighed on the other end of the phone. But I knew that already. She continued with ache in every syllable, "The rents are high, the neighborhoods are bad . . ." My insides were scorching, but I said nothing except "You think so?"

"There's no way," she said, "we can do this."

I listened with my life to her, to the mother words of my lost parent. Like a gambler running out of money, hoping for high returns, I had mortgaged my youth, anted up my newborn, bet on my mother's return; and I was losing bigger by the minute. I was still too much of a daughter to be a mother.

I called the Farrells within the next couple of days.

13

On June 7, I packed all Simone's things—her bassinet, the baby clothes my grandmother had shopped for, diapers, unused formula and bottles—and put them in the kitchen, close to the door. I said good-bye to the baby I had given birth to less than three weeks earlier, handed her to my grandmother, whose eyes I could not look at, and left the house. I cannot remember where I went or for how long, but when I returned, the kitchen was empty, and Simone was gone.

In a way, on that day the loss was harsher for my grandmother; she had bonded with Simone, and she had lost a chance to love a baby again. She took her sorrow in small doses during the weeks that followed, only, it seemed, when she had no choice; she'd dab her eyes with the corners of her apron, in front of the sink peering out the window as she did the dishes. She never knew I saw.

I was more prepared. Since that awful day in the doctor's office four months before, I had been conditioned by my dread, and I began then to retreat. I knew this might happen. I knew it could. So I stayed outside the experience, a foreigner in my skin, numbed by the dull buzz of a juvenile survival mantra: If I don't admit it exists, then I won't miss it when it goes. The baby who swam inside and pushed against me had been carried away, and I walked dazed through the motions.

I had made a baby to bring back my mother; if that didn't work, then nothing would. My mother did not know, it became ruthlessly obvious, how to stay. So at seventeen I was losing a daughter and mother forever, at the same time.

If my mother had called with hope, and a place to live; if my brother had warmed to the sight of the baby yarn; if my grandmother had expressed her yearning; if I had loved my boyfriend and he had had a job and a home; if I had been older and had money—would I have kept Simone? I don't know. It does not matter now.

Part II

Postpartum

14

In the year after I gave my daughter away, I fought the pull to reclaim her every heart-pounding second of every day. It was an exercise in a kind of restraint I never knew I had and have not experienced since. I refused to accept the fact that not only had I just given away my child, but that I had had a baby to begin with. It didn't happen. I used all the emotional energy I had access to to keep the truth of her disappearance out of my life and certainly out of the lives of the people who knew me. If anyone spoke the truth about what I had just done, I was prepared to lie.

Sometimes an irrepressible sorrow or fear eroded my stalwart refusal. I would go to bed at night determined to call the Farrells in the morning. I could not keep the battle up without losing life-threatening amounts of sleep and sanity. How could I have known that I would feel this way? No one told me I'd be hounded by a barrage of progressive imaginings—my baby at one month, her face at six weeks. Does she know I'm gone yet? I thought if I could just see and touch her I could wake up one day and go on. But seeing her would have unhinged me. I had made a deal that felt less like a promise than a pathetic default.

But I did not call. Eventually my urge to reclaim Simone went underground; I trained myself to ignore, often enough, a tug to go to her, to hear that she was healthy, that she was not in a corner somewhere tired-eyed and lonely, crying for the scent of her missing natural mother. Most of the time, I succeeded in eliminating her from conscious memory, but my suppression of the facts exacted a high price—emotionally, I had flatlined. I had forgotten how to cry, and knew I could not love. And I certainly didn't feel I ought to be loved. After a year, the hole left by her absence lapsed into a tolerable ache that for years made the day ahead feel slightly restless, as if I had forgotten something.

15

My infant intruder had left her mark. At seventeen my breasts
had been formed by the milk they had stored and then lost
and my abdomen had the curve of having cradled a newborn.
I had possessed the firmness of female youth too briefly, but
I did not blame my body. My mother had given me that. She
had declared, often enough and with zestful indignation, the
difference between the bodies of men and women. "We have
hips, Jan," she would say when I would spin out into an
adolescent, mirror-induced combustion. "Women are *supposed* to have hips."

And when I was young and wanted to know why I did not
have a penis, as my brother did, she smiled. "It's not that we
don't have penises; it's only that they wear their insides outside." So, it was a matter of style, I gathered.

Aside from wanting, since the age of ten, legs the length of
trees, I have never wanted anyone else's nose, hair, or breasts.
When I was a girl, my mother firmly forbade makeup, ear
piercing, hair tinting or perming, high heels, or nylons, not
from prudishness but because she wanted me to know that my
natural look surpassed any synthetic alteration thereof. Even
when the ultra-yellow-haired, pinched-waisted, buxom Bar-
bie doll became the mutated ideal of female beauty, I remained vain about my dark hair and green eyes, moderately

sized breasts and average ass. It was understood that all the rest of me—my sociability, humor, smartness, confidence—preceded the details of and, for the most part, informed my appearance.

So I had entered womanhood with a body that had been in privileged places, that had tried, labored, and succeeded in doing its best work. My body had become my secret souvenir.

My subconscious plan to deny the experience was easy enough. There was no proof. There was, simply, a lack of evidence to the contrary; in a group of my peers I did not have matching stories.

There was no prom, graduation, steady boyfriend, or outrageous ski trip, no getting caught by parents for anything, no being grounded, no driver's ed, no sweet sixteen party, no unbuttoned blouses on summer nights in the woods, no stupid parent stories. I went from kissing to gestating, from my first ride on the subway to my first apartment, from babysitting jobs to insurance company positions, from budding breasts to lactating breasts, from saving allowances to self-support.

At seventeen I was bluntly aware of my meager resources, financial and otherwise. Having no parents, only a brother at college on borrowed money and grandparents on a fixed income, made it clear exactly upon whom I could depend.

Now, I am not ungrateful for my hurried adulthood. Both my brother and I have a haughty self-reliance that enables us to be at home, unintimidated, in most of the adult world. Neither of us has required assertiveness training. We can turn a buck into a day's worth of food, and free time into a week's worth of plans. We clip coupons, travel cheap, wear our secondhand clothes until styles hit their second cycles, and regard impatiently the general inability of most people to get things done, swiftly and with order. We can live well on nothing. We are the worst of self-made men, and the best of capable allies to the people who know us. We are responsible with a fine-tuned vengeance. While on our own in our youth, we gathered a momentum of self-styled autonomy that has been hard to slow or stop and, for those who are closest, maddeningly impossible to live up to.

Looking back now, I feel as toughened by my busted-up youth as I am proud of having outlived it. But for years I hid a half a decade's worth of me.

16

Four weeks after I had Simone, at the age of seventeen, with one suitcase and one hundred dollars my grandmother had extracted from her modest savings, I left Benton to live and look for work in the city. I moved into the Franklin Square House, a rooming house for women in the South End of Boston, and after a week of interviews I was hired as a filing clerk at an insurance company. I would sit around the lunchroom table at work and listen to newlywed women pine for pregnancy and children. They would wonder what it was like, and I would wonder with them. I began the plan of lies. I denied the entire experience to everyone except the few who had eyewitness evidence of my bloated belly.

I even lied to my pediatrician.

I had decided to go to someone other than Dr. Bradford for birth control advice after I had my baby and before I moved to Boston; I already knew what he would say. After I had delivered Simone he hinted, in the hospital, at my possible salvation. "Now you know what you have to do," Dr. Bradford said after he asked about my episiotomy. "Wait. For marriage." He seemed to think that a nonvirginal girl could grow back her hymen if she promised to wait until a man made her a wife before losing her restraint again. So I went to Dr. Moses,★ who believed himself, on some level, the biblical equivalent of his name.

This doctor, a Humpty-Dumpty look-alike, became a rich man by settling into a small, uneducated town—Benton— and overprescribing for geriatric patients and pocketing comfortable fees as a company doctor with an ever-watchful eye on the bottom line.

After I sat down in his office, he pulled his suffering chair up close to me. As he sat, reeking of Old Spice, his immense middle burst over his belt and buried his thighs, nearly suffocating the bony gray knees that escaped from under his portly load. His glasses bobbed atop bloated cheeks every time he spoke. One hand landed on my knee and squeezed, as the other crawled across my shoulder until he flattened his fingertips against my throat and grunted, "Swallow." I want birth control pills is all, I had uttered meekly. He clicked his tongue and shook his head.

"You have no need for birth control," the doctor declared, abruptly ending his ad hoc examination. "You're not married. Wasn't being pregnant and then losing that baby lesson enough," he huffed, "to keep you from getting in trouble again? I won't do it," declared the righteous doctor.

I told my grandmother what he had said on our way out of his office, as we passed a row of flannel-shirted, coughing old men and white-haired women hunched over canes. She snapped, "Who is he to tell people how to act after what he's been doing with Mrs. Wheatley for the past year or so?" I should've sent my grandmother in to do business, I thought; or at least stated the obvious, which was, yes, it was lesson enough, that's why I'm here. Instead, humiliated, I put my sweater back on and left.

So after I had moved to Boston I went to Dr. Toch, my

longtime pediatrician and the only doctor I knew in the city, for an appointment to get birth control pills. He asked if there had been any changes since he had seen me last, which had been at least three years before my pregnancy. No, I said nervously, as I sat bare-breasted on the examining table in front of him, amid marionettes and undersized chairs. The tall, dark doctor, whose face was divided by a perfectly groomed handlebar mustache and dotted by piercing black eyes, leaned into me. "You have had a baby," he said, as he cradled my breasts in his hands. "The areola widens and gets br-r-r-rowner when you have a baby," he whispered in his unusually rounded German accent. Well, yes, I demurred. And I said the awful truth once, and asked abruptly about my blood pressure. After a full examination, and no more questions, he gave me a six-month supply of birth control pills.

17

I began, in the years following, to orchestrate a punishing life to quench a low-grade self-loathing. I felt unlovable and had no reason to believe otherwise at an age when reasons are desperately needed. An adult woman can hunt for and find her own value—she can graduate herself into importance. But during the shaky span from childhood to womanhood, a girl needs help in determining her worth—and no one can anoint her like her mother.

The emotional palsy that began after I had lost my family and given away my baby grew thicker in the three years that followed. Not only had I surrendered a daughter but I had lost my youth, my confidence, and the childhood plans about the adult I had hoped to become. When I dared to envision a future, it didn't exist.

I spent too much time with men who would help me hate myself. I put myself at risk, allowing lovers who did not know me to harm me—their assaults could, at least for the fiery night or impetuous hour, rouse the numbness that had overtaken me. I offered myself as bait to someone else's bruising temper and suffered satisfyingly tragic wounds. I was trapped in an R & B soundtrack, soulfully adrift, in tight crushed-velvet jumpsuits, multicolored makeup, platform shoes—play costumes of a woman aspirant. The cover-up was complete;

there was no traceable me. It is what I wanted. It is why I stayed.

Lorraine was my salvation more than once. We had been friends since we were three years old, but she had pulled away after I had given up my baby. Her son had been born two months after Simone (she had graduated from high school seven months pregnant), and she was uncomfortable with my postpregnant childlessness. It was too close. She thought that I would trade infant lore, mother stories, that I would join a gang of two at-home, baby-bound teenagers, and we would keep each other alive, in touch. Instead, I erased it and began again, leaving her to live out her young motherhood alone, estranged from her family, who turned away because she had married the black father of her baby.

"You will live with this for the rest of your life," she threatened, when she found out I had given my baby away. "I know I will," I shot back, as if I were familiar with some survival strategy for loss. After that we did not speak for over a year. Eventually, in a friendship that has lasted over forty years, we became close again, without, at first, discussing the adoption. Much later, after I had kept two children of my own, she apologized about judging me during what she said must've been a time when I needed friends more than ever. She speculated that jealousy may have been the motive; she'd felt trapped, and there I was free from motherhood. But I took her rejection as a matter of course back then; I was not mad at her for pushing me out of her life. It was, I thought, all a part of the sentence for the crime committed. It never occurred to me to defend my decision to her or anyone, not because I was sure about it but because I always assumed it was indefensible.

After we became friends again, Lorraine sheltered me when I was bruised, in danger, or without a home. I would go to the cluttered apartment she shared with her two babies and her husband and feel safe, though occasionally suffocated by her obligated young life. She kept my pursuers away from the door. When I was not running for cover, or dancing in the dark on high-heeled shoes, I was sitting on a secret that was bruising my insides.

My brother, who had held my confidence over the years, made annual visits to the Farrells for Wiffle Ball tournaments, soda bread sandwiches and dark beer, and long promenades through the garden, which outbloomed itself by the year and of which Daniel Farrell had become so proud. Every year, without exception, my brother became a furtive ambassador to the home of his lost niece, his sister's child.

The Farrells' adopted daughter was told early on that this visiting man was her birthmother's brother. She would watch my brother, study his eyes, listen closely, and step around his presence as if he were aglow; perched at his knee, she was ready to absorb messages, hints, anything about a connection only he had, which had become magically important to her. This was the person who not only knew but was related to her mother.

For the first few years after the adoption, the Farrells sent Christmas cards from all of their family, and I secretly wished they wouldn't. Their Christmas cheer seemed callous, but I know they never meant for me to feel bad, only remembered. I never wrote back.

Rarely, when I had the courage and knew he had visited, I would take days to brace myself and ask my brother for news of the baby who had been renamed Rebecca Anne Farrell. I sat, deceptively casual, listening as he confirmed her existence. He told me how smart and beautiful she was—always good things. But I was ticking, feeling that if I moved, or if he said the wrong thing, I would implode. I was deadly vulnerable, so in eleven years, even though I knew he could tell me, I asked about her only three times.

I had imagined her often. A beige girl with my nose. A young child with questioning eyes and a soft mouth. Once when I visited a museum near where I thought she lived and saw a brown-skinned girl about the age she would be, I followed her from room to room, keeping my eyes attached to her, barely aware of what must have looked like the peculiar behavior of a woman possessed. Finally the girl turned to look at me. When her black eyes caught my face, I could not move. I froze, and looked straight back, until she left the museum with her friends, all of them smiling uneasily at a woman they must've thought had never seen a brown girl before.

For three years I worked steadily in three different jobs, filing, answering phones, adding numbers, and getting nowhere except bored. By the time I turned twenty, I had grown weary of alphabetizing the invoices of accident victims at an insurance company and was terrified, finally, of living at risk. I was about to pass, if I wasn't careful, what I began to think of as the last exit from a bad dream.

One night in the big house I was renting for the winter with a friend and her husband, I was awakened from sleep by the soft-shoe scuff of sneaking footsteps. I recognized, against my bedroom door, the sprawling shadow of the man I had lived with and had recently moved away from. He said nothing and stepped lightly. I was hoping for the kind side of the explosive man I knew. As he inched, still silently, closer to my bed, I locked my body in a stiff line, bracing for the worst. He careened into the room, heaved his body onto mine, and shoved and slammed and pried apart my thighs. He huffed and spit threats into my ear. I pushed back, fighting the clumsy force of a tyrant in the dark, too embarrassed to yell for help, hobbled by my good manners. As he jerked against me, sour sweat smeared my face. I cried quietly as tears dripped into my ears, and I surrendered, limp, wet, and bruised. When he finished his rape, he zipped up his pants, adjusted his sweater, wiped the sweat from his neck, and left, as if he had just taken an engine out of a car, with difficulty but successfully.

One month later, when my friend and her husband separated and moved out of the house, I was left without a place to live. I moved back in with my violent boyfriend.

Within days after my move, I was determined to escape. What next, I thought, being hanged by my panty hose in the shower when no one's looking? Now I was making the most dangerous moves of all, waiting around for turning-point damage, because I wanted to turn, somewhere, soon. But I felt constrained by the years I had wasted. I was twenty years old, I had no high school diploma, no money, no family (my grandmother was widowed by now and in failing health), no driver's license—no choices. My brother, unaware of the details of my dark life, disagreed.

You will go to college, he wrote in regular missives of encouragement. Thanks for the vote, I said, but I have sixty-four dollars in the bank, I am a high school dropout, and I can't even remember how to read. He had applied to and been accepted by an expensive college and had learned how to creatively acquire loans, grants, and scholarships, so his letters contained detailed advice about what to say on college applications, and how to get money for school. He was on a mission; he would do what a brother could do to help restore his sister's sense of herself, without, of course, saying so.

My first application to college, launched with much resistance and many excuses, was turned down. It was what I expected, but my brother was indignant. Apply again, he said. So I did, reluctantly, sure of certain failure, miffed at having to fill out more forms and write more essays. Years later, I found out in fragments that, after I had been rejected the first time, my brother had stormed into the admissions office and made clear his shock at their bush-league failure to recognize his sister's brilliance and potential contributions to the college. Moreover, he urged, she is poor and needs money.

In November of 1972—two months later—I was admitted into the February semester with advanced standing (because of a high GED score) and a promise of a full four-year scholarship. It truly recharged my life.

I told only Lorraine and the woman at the insurance company to whom I had given my notice that I'd be going to school. I spent days dreaming about college in the country on a campus with trees, away from adding machines and dangerous men, and savored the secret as a reprieve. I packed one suitcase full of jeans, jerseys, and one pair of platform shoes (I left the heels and tight velvet pantsuits behind). Before dawn, on a below-zero mid-January Thursday, after staying awake most of the night, I quietly, slowly moved out of bed and out the door, picked up my bags, which I'd left at a friend's house the night before, and took off for the Trailways bus station. The man I lived with and was afraid of was sleeping, and he would find me gone in the morning. I was running for my life and never looking back.

18

The university was grown-up recess—sleeping until noon, staying up late, obligated for a mere few hours of the day, and finally having enough money to live on. (My grandmother had arranged through her friend the bank president for me and my brother to be recipients of college grants available from personal gifts through the local bank. As long as we stayed on the dean's list, there would be living money for us both.)

College was a perfect backdrop for renewal. I began to feel smart again and gorgeous for the first time. Thus began a slow resurrection of my girlhood confidence.

Friendships were easy, exhilarating in a way I had never known (I had been working with women who went to baby showers and Avon parties, who talked appliance price comparisons, women who had been married too long and lovelessly, or worked too much and hated their bosses). My grandmother visited with her friend Belle every other week and brought my favorite pies, banana bread, or cookies and a jar of the homemade chop suey she knew I loved. As my roommates and I unloaded the car, Nana, who knew no one in college except her grandchildren, boasted to Belle about her granddaughter's university A's and scholarly achievements.

I loved living with girls, the sisters I'd never had. We talked about shampoo, boys, books, played pinball, and crammed for sociology exams in the library smokers. We waitressed.

As the months went by, because I was a nontraditional student (three years older than most of my classmates), I found myself drawn to a core of instantly familiar female friends, most of whom belonged to an on-campus organization called DWHE (Disadvantaged Women for Higher Education). The group's members were single parents, whom the state had agreed to assist in their college education by helping to pay for books and child-care expenses and facilitating loans. Those at DWHE were a cohesive group of diverse, determined women who, for the most part, were ably handling motherhood, jobs, and school. I felt at times so comfortable with and invigorated by these women that I wanted to attend their meetings, but I had no child, a prerequisite for membership.

Susan, who had a daughter a year younger than the daughter I had lost, told me one day about a mutual friend, the mother of two sons, who had given away a baby when she was a teenager. I wonder, Susan posed, what that would be like? "Jesus," I said, "I can't imagine."

Two of my friends then, who are still close, were the mothers of daughters as old as Simone. About fifteen years later, when we all had families, I told them about the baby I gave away. They listened, never asking me to explain why I had kept the truth from them. Then we traded details.

Claudia,* who was unmarried, had decided she could not have an abortion, even though her boyfriend was unwilling and unready to be a father. Within twenty-four hours of her delivery, she told me, she found herself fighting off a needle-wielding nurse who had been instructed to puncture Claudia's breasts to dry up her useless milk. Useless, she was told, because of course she would have no baby to nurse. At twenty, and because it was and still is her nature to disprove the faithless, Claudia had the strength and anger to fight back.

A year later, our friend Karen,★ nineteen and unmarried, lost her twin daughters to Catholic Charities within hours after she had delivered them. Without the father, and disowned by her disapproving mother, Karen was alone in the hospital and gave in to the hard sell of the adoption agency: She would be selfish to keep them. Wouldn't she want her babies to be with a family who could buy the girls new shoes and give them a good life? Accepting the implication of her own endangering self-centeredness, Karen surrendered her babies, only to find herself, seven weeks later, literally racing to the agency to recover them. Recently, Karen confessed that the temporary severance from her daughters after their birth has never fully mended. She does not, she has said, love her girls the way she loves the child she had years later and kept from birth.

In the 1960s more babies were adopted than in any other decade in U.S. history, under circumstances those of us who were there have good reason to question. In a critically defenseless state, a young mother, frightened and doubtful about her abilities to handle the baby she has just accidentally had, succumbs too easily to the voices around her. In her postpartum daze, a young, ambivalent mother is prey to the disapproving and often acts with little regard for her own needs and desires.

Though I was most comfortable with the single-parent students at the university, I was glad not to have to hustle, as they all did, to find a baby-sitter every time I wanted to go out. I was relieved not to have to struggle with bills and the cost of books, and to have to arrange and rearrange schedules on a daily basis. I was consciously grateful for my unencumbered young adulthood. My success at college, busy social life, my two trips during summer breaks to San Francisco (hitchhiking the first time, with a carload of friends the second)—all of which I knew I would not have had the freedom to experience if I were a mother—convinced me I had done the right thing when I gave my baby to parents more prepared. My brother, on the rare occasions when we talked about it, reminded me that Simone's adoption, by people who we knew and trusted and who had wanted her, had been a happy fate.

Four years after I parted with Simone, during my second year of college, I began to see the sense in her having a family that was not me. I was thriving. My brother assured me she was too. For the first time, I let myself go forward because I knew I would never leave my sorrow and because, on some level, I knew my daughter and I were not finished.

This feeling—of our eventual confrontation—resided within me from the day I gave her away, primarily because of the Farrells' and my vague understanding that at some future date their daughter and I would meet, though we never articulated a plan. But, more deeply, I always sensed that a day would come when my daughter and I would fight it out and settle scores. While she was growing up, I'd be getting on until that time of reckoning.

When I was twenty-one, I was called at my apartment off campus by an attorney who said he had some papers for me to sign. Papers? Adoption papers, he said. Daniel Farrell had contacted him about my never having signed the surrender (the legal affirmation of my relinquishment of Simone). I felt found out, slammed. I didn't know who this man was, and a calculated oblivion had successfully erased from my memory the details surrounding the adoption, such as the legal necessities. Now I was being forced to confront the most final of details. When the lawyer asked if I wanted to read the form before signing, I snarled at him. No, I said. (Did he think I was enjoying this?) After I scribbled my name on the piece of paper in front of me, I darted out of his office on Main Street in the middle of my college town, feeling as if I had just bootlegged my soul.

In my second year of college, I was living with a man I loved, and I decided I wanted him to know about Simone. I tried at least a dozen times in three months to say it, to let him know without making it sound too *big*. Finally, on a Sunday in August while we were shopping flea markets, I got out of his pickup truck and blurted out the facts. He smiled, wondered what the joke was, had he missed something? No, really, I said, I had a baby and gave her away, but it worked out fine, I added (the necessary buffer). He stared at me and asked angrily why I hadn't told him before. He was mad at my foolish lack of trust in him to accept, simply, a part of my past. He hugged me and never brought the subject up.

I had endured the telling of it without falling apart, without being judged or pitied. It became a supremely rehabilitative moment. For the first time, someone outside the experience knew, and I did not faint from disclosure, or feel soiled or stupid. And he stayed.

19

After graduation in 1975, I headed for New York to take a job in the media (my degree was in journalism) and left my boyfriend and college behind, missing both enough to want to turn back three times in three months. Eventually, I was grateful for my promising position at a TV station and had fleeting fantasies about a high-powered career; but I fell in love with a sable-eyed man who worked in the art department, and my ambition was defused. When I had to choose between working in the studio until the early mornings of weekend days to get ahead or spending my time with him, the choice felt simple. Thomas showed me the deep, dreamy world of museums, salsa, and midnight cafés. And he had a way with kids. We traveled the streets of the city in each other's arms and spent hours in dark ethnic restaurants sipping strong coffee past midnight, considering Picasso's nudes and tenants' rights.

At age twenty-five, my biological clock was shimmying off the shelf, loudly and frantically reverberating within an eager off-duty mother waiting for her shift to begin. A lingering maternal impulse was beginning to distract, and having children became a matter of overwhelmingly unfinished business. Even before we spoke, I dreamed this artist and I would have two boys. I told him about Simone on our third date. It was getting easier.

Getting married, however, was never a part of the plan. When I was of marriageable age and with this man, there seemed an extreme lack of reasons to have a wedding. There was no family from whom to seek approval or respect or to risk embarrassing if I should live with a man and have babies without benefit of wedlock. If I had married and my parents (self-acclaimed Bohemians in their time) had been around, they might have felt, on the contrary, that they had lost their child—of whom they had expected an original sensibility—to thoughtless tradition. My grandmother was unfazed. She had been conditioned long ago by her daughter's aberrant conduct to endure surprises and in her late age was a seasoned forgiver. Having lived through interracial romances, hippie haircuts, her own daughter's baptismal boycott, and the teenage pregnancies of both her granddaughter and her daughter had inured her to the untraditional choices of her nongenetic relations. Her granddaughter's lack of matrimony was of no concern (though she would've loved the wedding, I'm sure). And though our friends occasionally suggested we invent a ritual to celebrate Thomas's and my union and future family, the idea never seemed to gather enough gusto to actually happen. We had a boisterous party instead, during which Thomas and I were showered with huge boxes of recirculated baby clothes, and handblown glass chalices.

Thomas and I moved out of the city, back to the country; I was looking for a suitable nest, among friends and trees, and close to a trusted midwife. But after suffering a slow, inevitable miscarriage two months following the move, we crashed. I became humiliated by the ironic cruelty of being denied a pregnancy I was finally ready for. You were given a chance once before and blew it, the tittering Fates suggested. The due date of this blighted pregnancy had been May 19, Simone's birthday.

But within a month I was pregnant again. The instant I found out I was going to be a mother, I felt invincible. This child beginning within seemed to inoculate me against harm and doubt and released a tide of courage and flight. At last, I was galloping across the finish line of a sloppy marathon I was weary of losing and wanted to end; I could stop racing after a mother who wouldn't stay. Being pregnant not only allowed but required me to leave behind a childhood that meant, in the end, emptiness. I was turning the corner to face my own children, eager to think of them instead of my own wasted wishes.

After my awful gynecological initiation at the callous hands of moralistic doctors, I sought a female midwife to help guide me through pregnancy and deliver my children. This time I would do it right, with a vengeance. My midwife, Judy Edwards, answered all my questions but was uninclined to coddle, told me how healthy I was, and made me feel during every visit as if I were in the throes of a commonplace miracle.

Immediately after the birth of my first son, when I was twenty-six, he was handed to me by his father in the delivery room. I cried so hard I thought this baby would not be safe in my arms. When I was pregnant and asked about gender preference, I always answered I didn't care but if pressed I'd want a boy, because, I realized much later, I had made a girl already. I held my boy, afraid of and fully grateful for each passing minute I was allowed to have him. When I was not looking at my new infant, I kept my eyes on his father, whose rejoicing and giddy pride helped make the moment real.

Within minutes after my son was born, I felt as if I had regained full use of my heart.

Less than a year later, I became pregnant again, even though we had little money, unreliable work, and a small apartment. When I showed up at the clinic with my six-month-old baby in my arms, the family-planning worker, who was familiar with my circumstances, lowered her head and told me I was pregnant. I cried, and she was sure she was the bearer of bad news.

"What are you going to do?" she asked with sympathy.

"God. I'm going to have a baby." I beamed through tears.

My mother, whom I had long given up as lost, appeared at my hospital bed after my second son was born. She came into my room with a basket of fruit and flowers and made a mild, awkward attempt to say the right things. The transcendent ecstasy of childbirth plus years of living without her had made my mother's halfhearted appearance sadly unimportant. She offered oblique condolences for my inability to produce a girl. It would have been nice, she said before leaving, to have had one of each, as she had.

I had always known I wanted two kids, close in age, based on the invaluable sibling world my brother and I (ten months apart) had shared. I wanted to give that to my kids, and, though we often had no money, I have never regretted the decision. The years of endless corn bread and soups, thrift-shop clothing, and low-income housing did not feel like years of struggle but a time of easy, immediate, and joyful purpose.

During their first months, Thomas confidently bathed his tiny sons as if he were polishing gems and changed their diapers as if he were packaging gold—with precision and respect. He prepared their baby food in jars he covered with whimsical labels created from pen and ink. One winter he designed and sewed a mobile of pastel satin tropical fish, which over the months fell from their threads into the crib below and eventually became stuffed toys.

While Thomas was at home watching the children and trying to make a living at art, I willingly worked as a cocktail waitress because the night shift gave me contented, albeit sleepy days with my young sons. Deprivation, of any kind, was far from what I felt.

During the first years of my sons' lives, I barely thought of Rebecca at all. I was fully engaged in the two lives I had just made and had become responsible for. The motherlove that arrived when Simone was born (and never left) was released and added to the love I gave my sons then and still do. With the children no one could take, my love was liberated and would be safe. It flowed.

When I did think of Rebecca, I thought of her in relation to them. She was a missing part of a new family. And for that reason, for my sons, I let myself think that meeting her would soon be possible.

20

For eleven years my foot had been plied to the closet door hiding a restless skeleton. But it was beginning to inch away, worn down by years of tedious restraint, gradually pried loose by the confidence of my motherhood. After I had had children of my own, I could feel secure (and tired) enough to tell the truth about Simone. I started with Amanda, a good listener and friend, my brother's girlfriend, after I had known her for three years.

I know, she said. I was stunned. She had been told years before by a friend who knew me in high school who assumed she knew, given my closeness with Amanda. But Amanda never told my brother she knew, and my brother told no one. Amanda had gone with him on one of his yearly visits to the Farrells, and their young adopted daughter had approached her.

Amanda told me that one Sunday months before, while the other adults talked loudly over ale, the Farrells' adopted daughter had found her ear and filled it with a chain of questions she had been storing for years. What is my mother like? Does she look like me? What are her other children like? Does she ever ask about me? Will I ever meet her? Amanda, in minutes, put the pieces of the story together: Rebecca's mother was me. Then Rebecca told Amanda that she had heard I did not want to meet her. And without thinking, because she didn't need to, she said, "No. That's not true."

"I probably had no right to say that," Amanda said recently, "but I had flashed instantly on the way you were with your kids, and I knew that just couldn't be true." Then Amanda managed to explain to the young girl at her side that, if it were true, it was probably because after seeing her I might not want to give her back.

My sons have requested their beginning stories since they were old enough to understand them. They want to hear for the thirtieth time how I was out dancing the night before my first son was born, how their father was the first to hold them both, seconds after their births, how I knew who they were before they appeared. I tell them how they careened inside and across my huge belly while raucously stretching, earning my older son his nickname of Skates. Their father reminds them of their minutes-old brilliance, passing the Apgar tests with scores of 9 and an unheard of perfect 10. My brother and Amanda have told them how they kept vigil in the hospital during my labor, my brother so nervous about the imminent birth of his nephew that after less than an hour he fell asleep in Amanda's lap, amid visiting friends and carefully hidden champagne. My sons know the stories well. Adoptees do not have the luxury of envisioning their celebrated births or inheriting prenatal names of affection. They often know nothing of their debuts, or to whom to go to find out.

I drifted, clutching my love for my sons for strength as Amanda recounted her afternoon with my birthdaughter. I dared to think it might be time. Within the next couple of weeks, I composed a letter to the Farrells, introducing the idea of a reunion with their daughter.

In the time it took to exchange two letters, our plans had been made. I chose my words carefully, with a single concern for the comfort and approval of my daughter's parents. This would be, ultimately, their decision, I wrote.

Their daughter had been away at a crafts fair with friends when my first letter arrived, but, wrote back her parents, we will tell her you've written because she has been waiting for this moment all her life. Their letters put me at ease, and I was assured that our reunion was what they had hoped for and expected all along.

I chose this time to meet my daughter because I wanted her to be a natural part of my children's lives. If she and I were going to meet, I did not want her to appear on their scene, in their home, in their childhood, as a long-hidden, aberrant relation. At the ages of one and two, they would hardly remember her meaningful debut; her presence could become part of their natural rhythms, having always been there. In a sense, I was giving my children to each other.

When I first told my sons about their sister, I brought them up to my room. As we sat on the bed, I began to explain a story I knew they couldn't understand. They squirmed and looked around the room and occasionally met my eyes; I asked them to try to listen, please, this was important. After fifteen minutes of being held in a conversation they seemed to sense was significant but, ultimately, a sidetrack to their play that morning, they motioned tentatively to the door. Could they go downstairs now? they wanted to know. Of course, I said.

This quiet conference was for me. I wanted to tell my children, in my words, no matter how incomprehensibly, that their mother had a daughter, that another child, their sister, existed. I told them they should know that the delayed arrival of another sibling would in no way change what we had, and that they should try to love her.

★　★　★

I went on a perfunctory confessional tour of those closest to me, speaking the facts, readying the environment for the imminent appearance of a daughter no one knew I had. The Secret had legs now; it was out of my hands. I had some explaining to do, and, difficult as it was, I knew it would be even harder, ludicrous and unfair, to have to make sense of this sudden daughter on the spot, in the tense presence of perplexed friends.

I began by telling Merrill. We had met when I was nineteen (she had gone to college with my brother), and we had felt an immediate, joined-at-the-soul kinship. Even so, I had not told her about my pregnancy or the subsequent adoption until after we had been best friends for over ten years. Recently I asked her what she remembered about my divulgence.

"Your brother took me to the Farrells once, years ago. He had told me a lot about Daniel, little about Linette and the kids. I think he may have mentioned that they had adopted a child. When we arrived the kids were asleep, so I did not see Rebecca until the next day. Linette had made a tiny pink silk dress with crystal beads sewn around the yoke for Rebecca. She said something about it looking nice with 'her skin.' And there was an oblique reference to a record they had gotten for Rebecca by some black artist, maybe Junior Walker. I didn't know until the next morning, when I saw her, that Rebecca was biracial. I didn't know until about eight years later that I had any immediate personal reason to be interested in this beautiful child.

"Linette, Rebecca, and I spent the day together—Rebecca was about three—a perfect, balanced day. We took walks in the woods, Rebecca wearing her new dress, her head wrapped in a colorful rag strip steeped in bug dope. Linette and I talked, looked at paintings she and Daniel had done, made a cake for the other kids (she always provided high tea for after school). I thought, 'Now this is what adult life should be—this is what it means to have a family,' the pace, the colors, the laughing.

"The day I learned who Rebecca was, you and I were in a restaurant. We were alone, both of us with small kids by now. I can't remember what we were talking about, something to do with high school culture, and I made some sweeping statement about the end of high school, forgetting or possibly not knowing you had left school.

" 'I left high school because I was pregnant,' you said. We had talked about abortion in the past, and I remember being taken aback that you had never shared that you had had this experience—no other option occurred to me until you told me that a family had adopted your baby. I told you about that visit to the Farrells, wanting to remember everything, astounded that we could be so close for so long and that I could not know this. And then doubly astounded—and touched—that your brother had held this confidence.

"The only other memory I have in the interim between the visit to the Farrells and this disclosure was at our graduation party [she and I had graduated from college in the same year], when a dark-skinned black man drove up, got out of his car, and walked toward you smiling. You froze; and your brother got between you and him and told him to leave. The threat and your brother's unambiguous, physical response to it were very palpable. I remember thinking two things: One, more than anything else in the world I wish I had a big brother who would defend me, and two, Who the Hell is this guy?"

But Merrill didn't ask, never knowing, in those days, where our confidences ended and my secrets began. The Waldrons, she knew, were very private people.

21

My mother used to say she didn't want to search for her natural parents because "this way I don't know who to hate," meaning her status as unaffiliated waif gave her cause to be truly egalitarian. Which she was.

But for many adoptees, there are desperate, internal stories whose origins and endings beg for resolution, before life itself can begin, no matter how loving or complete an adoptive family has been. In a sense, the inner lives of those who've been rearranged by adoption have nothing to do with the families who adopt.

The drive to seek and hold on to the truth of one's beginning exists only for the people essential to the moment of delivered life. When birthrelations search—and it is a search that has no beginning or end—the rest of the world disappears into the fuzzy outer edges of the focused pursuit. Even after we find, our reunions can be so consuming, alienating, and endless that every shared moment turns into a league of two that crowds out the company of others. Conspicuously hungry and tirelessly hopeful, birthrelations stalk their separated years, desperate to retract their losses.

My brother would drive me to her. He knew the way, and I couldn't imagine making this long, nervous trip with anyone else. It was July 13, 1980. Not much was said on the ride up. I wore a white pullover blouse I had made, a green skirt dotted with rose and blue flowers, and leather sandals. My ankles were locked for the hour and a half it took to get to the Farrells' rented white farmhouse. I remember only the sign that named her town and my brother cuing me, We'll be there in about fifteen minutes. I stared into the highway without seeing.

At her house, she fidgeted with her barrettes and hair ribbons, checked the mirror, went to the windows, looked up at her father, who watched over her with love on this day. When we pulled up, Rebecca saw our yellow car through the screen door, and at that moment Daniel announced to his daughter (she told me later), "Rebecca Farrell, this is your life," and she beamed tentatively.

The door squeaked open onto a sprawling forsythia bush, and there stood Linette and Daniel Farrell, and in between them their daughter, Rebecca, a vision in blue, with satin streamers in her coarse, curly hair. She would not take her eyes off me. Her parents, my brother, their house, the grass fused together in a cloud outside the circle of her. I moved to hug her, because that was what I was there to do, but I could barely stand. My knees, I feared, would fold and I would crash to the ground. We went into the house; adult voices rumbled in low tones far away.

Then we hugged. Rebecca's hold was calm; she seemed at home in my arms. For her (she said later), it was a "these were the arms I started in" embrace. I fumbled for the back of a chair the minute she broke away.

I saw no signs of me in her. She did not have my nose, or eyes. Her skin was buttery brown. I was white. She seemed shier than I imagined a girl of mine to be. More withdrawn. Is a mother's daughter meant to seem so unrelated? She retreated, hypnotized by this woman, her mother, while the grown-ups talked. This eleven-year-old stranger and I bore a tunnel between us, smiling, shocked, naked.

When I was aware of her parents, they seemed kind and relaxed, and I was in awe of their generosity—they asked if we wanted to be alone. I think I said yes, okay. I was eager to move out from the crowd. I left the house with a stranger. We went for a walk, down her country road to a drugstore where we ordered a vanilla milk shake that turned beige and flat. I explained (all the rehearsed rationale); I told her that giving her away was the first maternal act of my life, that I knew her parents would love her, and that I was too young to take care of her. But all I wanted to do was look at her. I wanted to inspect her until I knew by heart the length of all her fingers, until I could sort out her features—until I saw some of me. I wanted to memorize her.

Later Rebecca said all she wanted was to keep touching this long-awaited, often-imagined fairy birthmother of her dreams; if she kept her hand on my shoulder, or if our bodies were close, she would be all right, and I would not leave completely, again. We wanted to examine and handle each other, like terrified prey after escaping a predator's ugly chase.

Words were empty on this day. After twenty minutes of heavy pauses, we agreed to go back to her home. She tried more questions, about her father, about my sons, her brothers because, it seemed, they had been hanging in her head. I mouthed sentences she didn't seem to hear. Her voice was small and finally faded. We walked the rest of the way back on the sandy edge of her road in silence. We were hesitant strangers, who wanted to collapse into each other with grief.

Part III

The Reintegration Years: This Is NOT a Recovery Movement

22

After our reunion I waited. There was a letter or two, and some talk about this being a good time in Rebecca's life for me to reappear: Identity had become an issue, as is the wont for eleven-year-old girls, and I could help with that. But I expected nothing, did not allow myself to imagine the shape, or duration, of our places in each other's lives. I wanted to hear from my birthdaughter's parents—I was waiting for her mother to say something like "Hey, I'm the mother here." Then, at least, I would know what I was not.

Instead I heard from Rebecca. She wrote letters, in which she asked when could she visit next, and could I provide transportation one way? Still overwhelmed and exhausted by the demands of my own new motherhood, I attended nonetheless to the needs of my newest child, who seemed to adopt, with a grueling self-interest, a place in our family without a full understanding of what she was asking, and at what cost.

Reuniting with one's long-lost child is trying under the best of circumstances, but reuniting with an adolescent child is a supreme challenge. Adolescence is when child rearing gets tough; when, as parents, we have to say much that is neither fun nor popularly received. But the one factor, I have since learned with my kept children, that can soften and even pardon these labor-intensive middle years is our memory of them as our innocent young kids, of their soft feet and guile-less giggles, their beholden hearts. This chapter of Rebecca's life did not belong to me.

When our kids become teenagers, we spend much of our time issuing orders through gritted teeth, but at least by this time in our lives together our kids have memory banks filled with our gentle tolerance of an earlier time. They know we have not always been such hounders and naysayers. We the parents know they were not born exasperaters. We have shared history and mental maps with our kids, the good times, the bad times, the times period. Above all, because we the parents know our children, we know their awful stages are just that, stages. So assuming the instant family membership of an adolescent with whom there is no history becomes a disjointed challenge, because of a lack of the long view and a cultivated love.

Rebecca's debut in our house has since been reduced to and remembered as the Nike Incident.

During one of her visits, Rebecca made clear that she wanted a pair of new sneakers. Fine, I said. Even though there wasn't much money, we could manage that. Good, she said, a pair of Nikes was what she wanted and what she thought she ought to have. Her middle school was intensely fashion-conscious; she was the only black kid in her community and felt an inordinate pressure to conform, if only in dress and style, to ameliorate all the other differences between her and her classmates. With two small children, a waitressing job, and a tentatively employed partner, I did not even consider spending the money it would take to shoe this girl elegantly. Generic sneakers were what I could afford.

Rebecca could not fathom our refusal. With a lunge, she slammed onto the couch, banged her fists, threw pillows, and pleaded injustice. Her performance stunned us. She couldn't possibly wear any other kind of sneakers, she complained desperately. My sons' father and I, unaccustomed to preteen high drama, and not even slightly aware of the stakes of adolescent beau monde, laughed, incredulous, and Rebecca did not get Nike sneakers.

Having since witnessed my sons' experience in these matters, I understand how ruthless the edicts of peer fashion can be. And, in a way, Rebecca helped prepare me for this phase with them. When I started seeing signs of covetous sneaker tendencies, I was prepared to draw the line. I refused to buy full-priced billboard clothing, so my sons became bargain hunters. I would meet them halfway.

Rebecca, however, did not have my gradual parental knowledge to see her through her scene on the couch, her aching wish to conform. And adolescent outbursts, to the uninitiated, have the effect of bad opera; you're not sure whether you want to cry or laugh or leave. At the time, I knew of no other kids who anguished over shoes and jeans; my toddler sons were happy to wear thrift-shop sweaters and K mart boots, grateful in handmade britches. I simply did not know what do to with this girl's despair over shoes.

Nonetheless, we remember this scene as a kind of a getting-to-know-you moment, an incident that forecast a pattern between us. Rebecca's sense of entitlement—her assumption of guaranteed giving—and my constant edification of checkpoints and unwillingness to indulge expectations gone awry.

When Rebecca started to visit me, my two young sons, and their father, we lived in a small two-bedroom apartment. At first, she was happy enough to have brothers and felt comfortable around their father, but she was a girl on a mission. It was, eventually, obvious. She was coming to collect, and she wanted everyone who wasn't me out of the way. At her age, she did not have the savvy or the generosity to hide the fact.

Rebecca had a sense of little other than regaining a mother lost. She pouted or protested when friends came by, or when my kept kids needed more of me than she could have. She became a cranky two-year-old, stubbornly possessive, frantically intolerant of my divisible love. She dismissed my children's father by pretending not to hear him when he spoke.

I felt a tide of endless requests at my heels: Could I bring her shopping, could she have me for at least an hour, just us out to lunch? Could I sew her a skirt, in the colors she would pick out? She demanded all that I hadn't been and what she clearly knew she wanted me to be—another mother, the kind she already had.

I was uncomfortable when, after she had known me less than a month, she came to my house and opened the refrigerator, turned on the TV, and made long-distance phone calls without asking. It did not occur to her to say thank you or please, or to take her dish to the sink. She did not pick up after herself or share food without being asked. It had become uncomfortably clear that Rebecca had been brought up in a way that differed fundamentally from the way I had chosen to bring up my sons.

There was nothing about Rebecca that linked her to me. She did not seem a part of my skin, the way my sons did. Her flesh didn't melt into mine the way my sons' arms, heads, hands fell unconsciously into the arcs of my body. She could not translate the inflections in my voice—a serious warning, a gush of affection—the way my sons did within seconds. We had no common language. I was always aware of our physical separateness and became stiff and hesitant when close, as if some invisible shackle inhibited the impulse to touch. Was I afraid of revisiting the fusion that had been so violently disrupted years ago, when she was lifted from my belly during her first breaths? Or had she grown into a foreign object over time? Suddenly, there was a daughter in my house, and she didn't feel like mine.

23

Like many adoptees, Rebecca had dreamed about her lost mother, and I, she said later, had enough of what she had imagined to keep her beholden; I had become a romance figure, swelled to perfection in the mind of a daughter hungry for a hero. She was enamored with the possibility of reinventing the years lost and carrying on as if an adoption had not occurred. Through willful imitation, she assumed the rights (new sneakers and maternal access on demand) of a long-lost daughter; it would be as if I had never left, as if she were a lifetime tenant in my life and I in hers. I was flattered, guilty, and naive enough about being a parent to allow myself to be steered by her demands. She brought to me and my family an insistence on specialness.

The Christmas after we met, she wrote a story on squares of drawing paper, stapled them together to make a book called "The Best Day of My Life," and gave it to me as a present, with love I am sure. In it she wrote: "Now I think of Jan as a second mom." I was touched but overwhelmed, and not entirely sure I was ready, would know how, or would have the time to mother a third child, an adolescent girl.

We came to a common event—our reunion—with different perspectives and emotional license, by virtue of age and memory. Rebecca was realizing a dream she'd been having for several childhood years—finally meeting her mother. For me, this reunion meant confronting the result of a teenage error in the form of an eleven-year-old girl. Rebecca was free to gush and react, while I felt the need to stay presentably grown-up and steady even as my insides churned with doubt and vulnerability. In the early days, being with my newfound daughter often felt like smiling through a toothache.

When I had thought of meeting Rebecca, I did not, could not think past the huge, heart-pounding event of our first face-to-face meeting since the day she had disappeared from my grandmother's kitchen. I may have given in to an image of me, her peripheral aunt, and she, my joyful, young companion, spending a summer week together, laughing on the shore in bare feet, in tans and towels, happily reconnected, our dark ordeal a distant memory; and then, I knew, she would easily return to her mother and father, the parents in charge. I thought the fault line between us would fade seamlessly with time, and we would rejoice in days of play after the storm. We would regain each other, the best of our light-hearted selves. But mostly I only hoped she would not shake her nubile brown finger in my face and blame me, through a sobbing rage, for ruining her life, for delivering her into abandonment.

I had no formal ideas about what kind of relationship we would have or where it would go. And Rebecca's adoptive parents and I did not talk about it. They presumed a relationship between me and their daughter, giving the blood bond far more significance than I ever dared to presume or thought possible. I wanted to know the rules. I wanted a map to this child—what did she love, hate, did she have a temper, what were her moods, did she like spaghetti and sleep easily, did she have any allergies? Did she think I was a monster? What had they told her? What did she know?

I wanted a primer for mothering a reclaimed child. Instead, in faith, her parents granted me maternal amnesty and an unwieldy field of influence. Probably because we wanted to trust the natural course of our hearts, as we had done from the beginning, and because we didn't know what to say or how to begin to say it, we avoided the obvious questions.

Daniel or Linette and I would arrange transportation, meet in midway parking lots, sit and wait for the other in warm running cars, and cross paths as unlikely bicustodial parents doing what's best for the kid in the middle. The Farrells and I would hug, promise to get together for dinner sometime soon (we never did), and talk about the general flow of daily life, briefly. We walked around the subject of Rebecca. Then we would exchange her. I would hug her good-bye (or in greeting) under the eyes of her parents, who seemed to turn away. Then we would get in our respective cars and drive in opposite directions. We were not unfriendly.

Afterward, I would feel as if the Farrells had dropped off a complex piece of machinery I had not ordered but felt lucky to have, whose operating manual had not been included. They had left me, a related stranger, with the care of their cherished child, for whom I did not yet feel love but only supreme confusion jammed with emotional leftovers I could not even begin to sort out.

We never tapped the inevitable reserve of nervous questions we had about each other, about their daughter, my baby, our fated paths of years ago, and the hidden turns in the road ahead. We didn't then and haven't since told each other how completely we must have trusted each other, and how profoundly thankful we are for each other's parts in our lives.

Among cocreators of children, there is a unique point of

view, a seventh sense toward the children; there is a secret territory of common language that only parents of the same children seem to travel. When spoken to outsiders, that language sounds indulgent, foolish even. Mutual children can provide a rare communion for their creators. In a sense, the Farrells and I held those common feelings for Rebecca, whom, from the moment of our reunion we assumed we would keep safe and love, separately but together.

But we were cordial instead, chronically inexpressive about our worries. They must have wondered, Was I taking Rebecca back? How much of her was I expecting to keep? Would their daughter begin to love me more than them? What should I give their daughter? What should I expect in return? Did I feel resentful of or threatened by them? I desperately wanted help with this but still felt like the criminal factor, unentitled to a full hearing of the circumstances that had merged our lives, again.

Rebecca's mother was always as kind to me as she was when she had visited me in the hospital the day after Rebecca was born. This time, though, her understanding and calm left me uneasy. I was confused by her carte blanche acceptance of her adopted daughter's clinging infatuation with me. Even if Linette and Daniel had accepted the inevitable reunion between their daughter and me, how do you prepare a place in your life for your child's mother? I ask myself this often while thinking of my kept children, and each time I am too destroyed by the question to get to the answer.

So while I tried to make up for years lost and Rebecca adopted me back with a vengeance, I kept a stern vigil for her mother's view. I acted, often at Rebecca's expense, on behalf of her mother, aligned more with Linette's maternity than with her daughter's demands, by explaining a parent's point of view when Rebecca complained about or questioned her parents. I was—haltingly, apologetically—as much a mother to Rebecca as I thought her other mother could bear.

As she was turning twelve, Rebecca's parents, having married young, had discovered a consuming social life. Their biological teenage children were independent enough, but Rebecca was not ready to be on her own. Rebecca worried that her parents' shift in attentions would make them less available to her, and she would be left behind, again.

The Farrells asked me to write to their daughter to explain; she might listen to me. But I did not understand it myself. My childhood had died on the vine at this age too. I had not been granted the privilege of acting out and against an immovable adult presence—my parents, deep in their own turmoil, were acting out instead. And now I was being asked to explain a kind of parental absence I found indefensible and bitterly familiar, though I am certain the Farrells could not know this. I wrote a letter, every word against my will, for Rebecca.

So my contribution to her life, at the age at which I had been left and lost, grew in importance over the first few years after our reunion. My ideas of us disintegrated under the urgent heap of her need. Turning away now would mean I had agreed to pass on the poison. Rebecca's parents handed her over with loving hope and then receded.

I fumbled with the implied mandate to fill in as Rebecca's primary guardian.

I moved through our relationship, on the outskirts of my instincts, uncertain about loving a child I had left, nervous about mothering another mother's daughter. In those years, my relationship with Rebecca felt indecently experimental. When I hugged her, I didn't feel it. When I counseled her, it felt more like dutiful tutelage than spirited parenthood. I was not happy or sad when I knew she was coming for a visit, and I could never be sure whether I was holding back, afraid of releasing a motherly love I was entitled to, or trying to siphon an empty reserve. I was driven by raw guilt and the tail end of a prolonged numb out; so my course with her was determined by a plan to correct my mistake. I would prove my decency to the girl I gave up.

But what I knew of mother and daughter love was nowhere near to what I felt for Rebecca. I searched her face and body for angles and colors I could match to my own. I begged for some palpable magnetic urge to bring her into me and keep her there, something close to the death-defying, sheltering instinct I felt for my young sons.

I knew I would try to do the right thing, but I could not figure out what was right to feel. And there were no books, advice, experts, or studies to turn to to find out what to call this union or how to represent the reasons we knew each other. I knew one thing, I told myself: I did not love her the way I loved my kept kids.

Bullied by guilt and bereft of know-how, I flopped about and was yanked into providing emotional first aid for us both, again and again. I began to chase Rebecca's cues and triple-guessed my handling of her needs. I filtered my advice before going to her with it. (Would I say something that would trigger the awful rejection she had been born into, which I alone had caused? Would I repeat my mother's crime of turning away? Would I prove the press about cold women who give away babies?) All of what I said and did had to be clinically faultless, tempered by adequate doses of maternal remorse and shame.

But it wasn't just my daughter I was dealing with. I saw the pain of my mother's adoption in Rebecca's pleading face. For all the adoptees in my world, I would be the birthmother who came back and took the heat. And Rebecca knew it. She faulted me at every turn for my fierce mismanagement of her feelings. Any adolescent girl would. But Rebecca had a perfect construct for the attack—an impeachable mother who could not deny the ultimate offense of abandonment. She blamed. I absorbed.

24

While I was trying to sort out the inner disorder of identifying Rebecca, she and I were left with the outer story to explain. Presenting her was and continues to be hard work. How to introduce a daughter who essentially has been deprived of the social, historical, and emotional connection the word implies? A daughter, but not a daughter, if you know what I mean. But no one ever does. Adoptionspeak—birthdaughter, searching, real parent, reunion, open adoption—can become a knotty snag in an otherwise smooth conversation. And there are still an unnerving number of people who have never heard the words—oddly, words that describe millions of people in this country. Chitchat converts into sputtering small talk while listeners scurry to find exits out of the threatening darkness of melodrama when the words or stories come up— they change the subject, test an array of facial expressions, or utter generic comments such as "How nice."

Once while writing this book I was asked what I was writing about.

"Adoption," I answered. I could never find a medium-sized response to this question. A blunt answer never told the true story; a longer synopsis was almost always required.

"Oh, I have friends who are adoptive moms," this suburban mother of four said, assuming I was one.

"Uh huh. I'm a birthmother, though, and that's what I'm writing about."

"Oh, I think that's wonderful. That's what *I* should be," she giggled, insinuating her fertility.

She must have thought a birthmother was a surrogate mother, a woman who plans to lose her child; maybe she could not imagine for the moment that I, of higher education and apparent financial comfort, could have given up a baby under circumstances less arranged. Or maybe she was fumbling for a benign, forgiving response. Should I have told her that what I had been—a groping teenager caught in a jam— was not what anyone should be; or suggested my committed opposition to women willing to rent their wombs, and then watched her squirm? I smiled and said nothing.

The spoken words are so tragically, hilariously estranged from the actual experience, it feels both frivolous and deadly to say them. And it just doesn't get easier.

But Rebecca and I continue to be befuddled, so it would figure others would be too. We have spent too much time stumbling through the protocol, trying to translate ourselves not only to ourselves and to each other but to the world at large. In the first years, all the information we came up with was fake. Briefly she called me Mom (and still does when speaking with her brothers) and called herself Rebecca Waldron. There were times when she thought of changing her name back to the original; she felt less like a Rebecca, she would say, than a Simone. I would introduce her as my daughter. She would say I was her mother. We were trying to come up with answers, but we barely knew the questions, so we fudged, fibbed, and tested.

When I was asked how many children I had, I struggled. I did a quick, nervous survey of my emotional and ethical obligations to the legions who seemed to have a stake in my answer; and I argued with myself, each and every time, about what makes a mother, when a child is a daughter. Sometimes I wanted to say three, but that is not exactly right. I've birthed three babies, I have two children. I've mothered them all. But my sons are my kids. Rebecca is my birthdaughter. In the end it rarely matters what I say, the answer always confounds and feels only marginally right.

"She's my daughter, but she was adopted, no, I didn't adopt her, I gave her up, we met, again, when she was eleven. I helped raise her, I know her adoptive parents, we were friends. . . ." I stammer, trying to cram two irregular lifetimes and an odd relationship into a three-second package for people who are often strangers, who may not care, who hardly asked for this detour into summarized true confessions. I try to sound matter-of-fact as I part with words that feel like tiny under-the-skin explosions and heart-stopping truths, no matter how often I speak them.

And it is always an awkward moment because of the personal stories so swiftly revealed. People know within seconds of my introduction of Rebecca as my birthdaughter that I lost my virginity when young, that the man with whom I slept and got pregnant was black, that I gave away the baby, met her again, and now have a relationship with the once infant I left. That is more than I care for people who barely know me to know. When I introduce my sons, nothing is revealed other than that at a reasonable age I probably followed the usual course to get them.

"I thought you had two sons?" a co-worker once said, after Rebecca visited me at work and introduced herself as my daughter.

"I do."

"But she said she was your daughter."

"She is. Okay. She's my birthdaughter." Silence. More

silence. My co-worker looked at me speechlessly, squinting her eyes, uncertain.

"Do you know what that is?" I asked.

"Yeah. Kind of. You gave birth to her."

I sighed, anticipating the unfolding of the saga, exhausted before I could begin.

"It's okay," she said sympathetically. "You don't have to go into it."

At this point, I had to get into it, unwilling to settle for anyone else's translation of *my* facts.

"Well, yes. I gave birth to her, and then she was adopted, and then we met again." The awkwardness had risen to new heights after I said this. She gazed dead serious into my eyes, as if I were a slow-ticking time bomb, aggrieved to the point of politeness. I'm used to the story but can't seem to get used to the telling of it, and I'm never sure how this all sounds to the uninitiated. I wonder if I'm starting to sound like a tragic buffoon, or like I'm trying too hard to trivialize what clearly must have been traumatic, and therefore end up sounding even more traumatized.

I often end my presentation by smiling, wanting to reassure those who have heard the uneasy truth of Rebecca and me that I will not require sedatives or resuscitation anytime soon, and that I do not bellow in the dark "What have I done? I am a pitiful fiend!" when no one is listening. "I have survived it," I want to say. "No sweat." Which is only half right. I have survived it, but it has been and continues to be an exhausting, sweaty ordeal.

For a while, I had decided, I would be committed to using the language. I'd introduce Rebecca as my birthchild and take a chance. If people are familiar with the term, they often appreciate the frankness. If the word is new to them, they seem to think I have said something mysteriously obstetric, as if this daughter had an unorthodox delivery or a rare defect. Then I explain the word and our relationship, in three sentences or fewer.

If we keep saying the words, as naturally and loudly and as often as we would the names of other family members, such as stepdaughter or niece, I reasoned, then the language will grow familiar to us, and so will the idea. But it is understandable why almost no one uses the language of birthrelations: When we do, we are delivering the first line of a tumbling, complicated story. And on most days it takes excessive fortitude to achieve a reasonable emotional distance in order to continue or explain.

Until recently, because hiding the identity of birthmothers has been the first step of a pervasive legal cover-up, it has not only been easy but expected for the natural mother to avoid her true story. There is no single factor that compels her to reveal herself, other than the reappearance of the grown given-away baby. Other than the undeniable presence of a birthchild, which open adoptions are likely to encourage, there is no visible defect, affect, or indication of a woman having had a baby she gave away. She can lie; it is hoped, often, that she will—it's less messy, really, for everybody.

Sometimes I follow the example of my children, who have more kinds of relatives than I, as a child, ever knew existed. They have halfbrothers and halfsisters, stepsisters and stepbrothers, a stepmother they call Tita, double cousins, aunts once removed, and uncles that aren't. Almost always when they are referring to any one of them, they drop the specifying prefix, or the qualifying details. Brothers are brothers, an aunt is an aunt. Sometimes my sons refer to me and their stepfather (whom they call Dave), as their parents; their friends know what they mean. When my kids refer to the members of the mosaic that is their family, the route by which all these people became relatives seems beside the point, petty even.

So some of the time, depending on my mood, I keep it simple and omit the qualifiers: Rebecca and I are a mother and her daughter. I have given up scanning those in my company for indicators, such as: What are they prepared to hear? How much do they know about birthrelations? I used to make it my work to measure the level of understanding in my listeners and then offer doses of an experience so prevalent yet so rarely spoken about. Most of the time, I speak the facts and let them stand. Rebecca is my birthdaughter, I am her birthmother.

25

My grandmother died in the spring of 1984, four years after I had reunited with Rebecca.

Two years earlier, when she could no longer live alone and there was no one left to care for her, I had taken Nana to a nursing home. The generation that would logically have assumed her care was missing. By the time my brother and I had families of our own, we had been responsible for, to some degree, our parents, ourselves and each other, and our grandmother, financially and otherwise. My brother had just become the father of a second baby and lived two states away, and I had become the single parent of two young sons. Our grandmother was incontinent, had to be lifted in and out of bed, and had fallen more than once when alone. But even if we had had the resources and physical strength to tend our grandmother, being baby-sat by her grandchildren would have been a mortal embarrassment to the woman who had carried the troubles of so many for so long.

We trudged down a narrow gray sidewalk under bony November trees in a skin-piercing cold, me carrying a suitcase filled with the only possessions left in her life—an estate reduced to a few dresses, photographs, stockings and underwear, clip-on pearl earrings, and one pair of brown canvas crisscross house shoes. She followed slowly and wordlessly in her bulky, big-buttoned gray coat, knowing almost that she was headed into days during which the kind of pudding served was pivotal and sponge baths would become her single pleasure.

I had not visited her enough when she was in the nursing home. The sour smells of sickness and rot, the lonely cries of dying people, and the sight of my grandmother so beholden, so out of place, nauseated me. It took me weeks to prepare for a visit, and weeks to recover. She was alone, scared, getting weaker and more melancholy every day she spent in geriatric captivity. In the last year of her life she had fallen and broken her hip; she stayed in a wheelchair, refused physical therapy, and surrendered. She was given an antidepressant. My stoic, steady grandmother was on a mood-altering drug, and that meant, for her, life-threatening despair.

My grandmother had survived all her relatives, all ten siblings, dozens of cousins, and most of her friends. That she outlasted them all, when genetic heart disease had killed all but one member of her immediate family at ages younger, some by decades, than she, is a tribute to her will. She had been fifty to a hundred pounds overweight most of her life, had a taste for white bread, sugar, and fat-fried donuts, and never got enough sleep. Simple logic dictated early death, yet she stayed on until the last one fell. An earlier death, at least, would have spared her having to be the charge of people more capable than she. That was her job, the original Caretaker Deluxe, and she was humiliated to have to count on others. She was sure she did not want to live that long. "I don't mind if I have my health, but I want to go before I'm a nuisance," she would say often before she moved out of her own house. But after she gave up her home, she never said it again, humbled by her dreaded dependence.

The nursing home called when she lapsed into a coma on

a Saturday night in May of '84. I located my brother and mother and told them that, if they wanted to, now was the time to say good-bye. We convened at her bed and stood together, for the first time in years, studying our dying matriarch, jarred every now and again by an irregular exhale, as if it might be her last. My mother, whose appearance was brief and detached, left the room. My brother asked for time alone with his grandmother. When he came out, I visited with her. In her darkened room, I was spooked by the hovering presence of death and felt embarrassed for her in her faded pink nightgown, without her wig (which she had worn in later years to cover her thinning hair). I wanted her to see us all together, one last time. She would have loved that; it was so rare and so hoped for. That night my mother had little to say and took the first available bus back to Boston, where she had been living since her return from her years on the road.

When my grandmother died two days later, at the age of eighty-two, I made a call to the funeral director, who asked if I could come and pick out a casket. When I arrived at the funeral home, the soft-spoken director in his dark, slightly small suit and sparkly tiepin, the soft Muzak, the shiny brass lamps, the dense oxblood carpets, the absence of, well, life, lulled me into a mode mournful, yet reverent of death. I was ready to spring for the top of the line, a white fiberglass tomb with intricate gold fixtures, to give my grandmother the splendor she so deserved and was never able to afford while living—a fancy postmortem for the Grand Matron. Finances, however, prohibited anything more reverent than a simple gray coffin. And besides, my grandmother had stated several times to my brother and me that she was definitely into a no-frills afterlife. No point, she said. Heaven is Heaven, and the soul's the only thing that's going anyway.

There were no funeral arrangements per se. The director

asked me to compose an obituary and to get a dress for my grandmother. On a sunny day in late spring, my young sons and I took a ride up to the cemetery to meet the director, who would then, with help, lower her body into the ground. All of her Benton family and friends had grown reclusively feeble in trailers on the outskirts of town, or had died years ago; no one knew where she had been during her final withering years—and visits from obligated semistrangers, with half-hearted condolences and canned cookies, did not matter to her. So on the occasion of her death there seemed to be no one left to tell. We spotted the black hearse parked near my grandfather's grave, got out of the car, and greeted the somber yet slightly enthusiastic undertaker, preparing for his finale in front of a graveside crowd of three.

Would I like to view the body one more time? Before I could decide about a final glance (Should my young kids see a dead person? Did I want to see her this way?), he had flipped the top of the casket back, revealing a calm, bespectacled old woman with closed eyes and smudged lipstick, reposing in a bath of white satin, her crooked hands crossed on a hollow chest. My sons stared, I watched them for signs of sickness or shock, and nodded quickly to the undertaker to close the coffin. I held on to my small children, and they held back, as my grandmother entered the soft spring ground, next to her husband, across the row from her sister Margaret, and in the middle of most of her brothers.

Years after, I asked Rebecca if I had ever taken her to meet my grandmother. I could not remember. She said, "Oh, yeah," and she remembered it well. She had first spotted Altie sitting on the front porch of the house in Benton, her wig askew, taking nails out of wooden lathing. (My brother was insulating the house, and this was Nana's busywork—assigned to keep her out of the way.)

Rebecca said that before we had gone into the house I told her that my grandmother would probably not understand who she was and that I was not going to even try to explain. Altie was dazed much of the time by then, forgetful and lost, but her long-term recall was often lucid and detailed. I would introduce Rebecca simply as Rebecca. (My grandmother did not know Simone's new name, and I had never mentioned that I had reunited with her.) Rebecca said she felt "weird" that day, not knowing who she should be, afraid of saying the wrong thing.

Still, after years of knowing Rebecca, I was intimidated by the truth. I was afraid that my grandmother's reaction might be inappropriate, hurtful, that she, in her sloppy, failing mind, could say something devastating or painfully honest to Rebecca, or me; that my grandmother, worn out by her years, would begin to sob and clutch her long-lost brown baby and I would scream and surely go mad.

So our visit that day was suspended by secrecy and hypocrisy. In sparing Rebecca and my grandmother what I thought could have been an unbearable scene, I squandered what would become the only chance for an exalted moment in the lives of both: a full-circle reunion for my grandmother with her great-grandchild. And I denied Rebecca the memory, the recognition, and the expression, in her own fourteen-year-old way, of gratitude for the woman who loved her first.

26

Shortly after my grandmother died, Rebecca and my mother crossed paths for the first and last time. We were convening in the foyer of a McDonald's restaurant somewhere in Boston, I corralling two young kids, Rebecca and my mother standing awkwardly outside the chaos. My mother had taken my older son to a Chinese restaurant for his fifth birthday and taught him how to eat with chopsticks; Rebecca, my younger son, and I were meeting them so I could take my five-year-old home. My mother seemed irritated in Rebecca's presence. I could not deduce why. Did she disapprove of the reunion? Did she think it unfair to the adoptive parents—had I no right to do this? Was her reunion with Rebecca a horrible kind of irony? She departed abruptly amid the noise, leaving me alone in the middle of my children—the grandchildren I had offered and hoped she would love, just as I had made Rebecca for her years ago. But again, she walked away.

Before that, we had talked about Rebecca only once. Annoyed after a tiff over the phone with my birthdaughter, I had stormed out of the house into the car, where my mother had been waiting. I was complaining, mother to mother, about the demands of my inherited adolescent. She listened and became uncharacteristically silent. I was sure she would understand my impatience with Rebecca's spoiled ways; I expected her outrage too. But she bypassed my point of view, and, after an awkward pause, she decided to speak. "Adoptees are especially sensitive about rejection," she said in support of her granddaughter. "Be careful with her."

27

I separated from the father of my sons in 1984. For the next three years, Rebecca and I became partners. We had each other. There was a vacant place beside me, and my lost daughter found it and settled in. Her brothers and I became accustomed to her, and I valued her company and help during a transitional time for me and in the lives of my sons. She visited often, most weekends, and all of several summers during the years I was a single parent, when she was fifteen, sixteen, and seventeen. She baby-sat, did errands, helped keep the kids on track. She began to give back, emerging from her self-involved preteen years. When she gave she glowed, she was out of herself and in the moment, unfettered by her nagging hunger for the lost years; she became proud of her ability to be generous. She was getting what she needed, her unencumbered mother, and I grew attached to her, for the first time. And I began to love her. A lot.

During these years, she was becoming interested in boys, so I did what I could to help. When she wanted to go to a teen dance club, I went with her and sat unobtrusively on carpeted bleachers in the dark while she danced. I tried to look un-motherly, yet not quite the girlfriend, scanned the room for people she might know, and passed on the goings-on I thought might matter—like who danced with whom, and which boys had noticed her. It was a giddy regression for me and, for her, girlfriend surrogacy of the sort so helpful in teenage society.

Each year we basked more in our alikeness—her laugh was mine, her humor familiar, we both loved to dance. We were annoyed and amazed by her brothers, my sons. I would start supper, the phone would ring, and Rebecca would pick up the knife and keep chopping the carrots. The kids would yell, "Mom!" but I would be busy. Rebecca would say, "What is it?" and they would go to her for help. Our home hummed with matriarchal order, and our boys were happily answerable to us, the women of the house.

We sunned on the back porch, put speakers in the windows, and gabbed about neighbors, clothes, and boys; we aerobicized to the erotic pleas of Teddy Pendergrass and the poetry of Stevie Wonder. We made excessively chocolate desserts and joked about our alleged diets until we collapsed into hysterics over our mutual thigh concerns as we spoon-fed each other seconds. She wore my clothes, and I struggled into hers; we filled out her college applications, talked about her dreams.

And we talked about hair. I brought her to Merna, a middle-aged black woman preacher who owned and operated our town's only black hair salon, a worn-down wooden room that tilted on the sandy shoulder of a busy street. Rebecca walked slowly into the tiny salon, where black men and women waited on metal chairs shoulder to shoulder and talked church and business through the thick smell of hair chemicals. Merna talked fast and constantly while she hot-ironed a customer's hair, and looked up to see Rebecca, a shy newcomer, standing on the outside of the heat and chatter.

When Merna finally got to Rebecca, she said, "Girl,

who's been combin' your hair?" (Rebecca later said she hated when people touched her hair, much less brushed it, because "they didn't know *how* to touch it. I knew that instinctively. I knew my hair wasn't like anybody else's, and no one knew what to do with it. It was just there, my nappy ole hair, going every which way.") And then, without missing a word of church talk, Merna tamed Rebecca's knotty curls with unself-conscious affection, yanking and stroking her hair as if it were her own. Merna combed, cut, and conditioned fourteen years' worth of mingled friz, and after two hours Rebecca was free from tangles, her curls released at least.

We were the closest to comfort during those years that we've ever come.

My friend Merrill recalled, "I remember seeing you run around together like girlfriends cruising on a summer evening, or the times when you stood up for her, and feeling jealous almost. I thought, 'So this is what it's like to have a daughter.' And then there were other times when there was no peace between you, when you would almost plaintively say to me (like when you were hunting for colleges or doctors for her): 'I wanted two kids because that is what I thought I could responsibly handle,' sighing at being drawn into this more historically complex relationship."

On my first date with David, Rebecca picked out what I should wear, smelled my mouth to see if there was evidence of smoking (I didn't want him to know); she blended my makeup and calmed my jitters. She told me I looked ravishing, assured me that she'd get the kids to bed at a reasonable hour, and that she'd clean up. I couldn't think straight, and she offered the best of levelheaded encouragement and cheer.

She waited up (I had hoped she would) and wanted to hear all. I told her David and I had kissed on the beach, and Rebecca and I swooned together.

But when I grew closer to this man, Rebecca watched her time with me shrink. The place beside me filled up, and she felt abandoned, again. As my romance bloomed, she grew panicky, as if she were losing oxygen. She was curt with David and became critical of our relationship; she was convinced that I and this new man were wrong for each other, even though she saw me happier than ever.

In the preadolescence of our ongoing reunion, Rebecca got mad. She was eighteen, but going on nine in so many ways. If this is so good, then why couldn't it have been from the start and why can't it continue to be? she began to ask with every breath. A golden era was lost again.

In 1987 Rebecca attended the college I had gone to fifteen years earlier. Her classmates were mostly blond skiers, and her teachers, with one exception, were white. When the school held a Diversity Day conference in the beginning of her second year, Rebecca was to be a featured speaker, by virtue of her appearance (and not necessarily her experience) and the dearth of otherwise qualified (i.e., diverse) guests. At nineteen she was easily seduced by other people's perceptions of her. The school newspaper interviewed her, and the story appeared on the front page. I was doing graduate work at the same college at the time and remembered the day the article, with Rebecca's photo, came out. Merrill, who worked on campus, remembered it too.

"I walked into some campus office and saw the paper with Rebecca's story: 'Her mother, impregnated by a black man ten years her senior, gave the baby up for adoption.' I remember my eyes burning, picking up that stack of papers and wondering for one crazy second if I could pick up and destroy all the copies out on campus. It seemed so reductionist, you presented as so victimized—and after all the years you had held this in.

"I wanted to call Rebecca and say: 'To you this is an interesting movie where you are the star. The supporting cast, however, has had years of sacrifice and hurt and made choices that right or wrong are not yours to violate.' It was the predictability of the story, the lack of richness that got to me the most."

I was destroyed when I read it too, but I did not confront her. I could not fault her, I reasoned, for telling the truth. But Rebecca seemed so willing to expose the story I had barely begun to tell. I did not want my part of the drama reduced to what I was sure would be perceived as a stereotypical disaster (white teenager violated by older black man) in most of the minds of our all-white college community. I didn't want to believe that she had not considered my anguish, my privacy, or the fact that my colleagues would read the story too. At her age, I had been irrationally protective of my mother, her kindest agent. The voice in this front-page confession was not the voice of a daughter; not mine, anyway.

Shortly after David had become part of my life, Rebecca, poised for further disappointment, suffered an eye-opening event, one she would say later shocked her into confronting a fierce fact. One snowy January night, Rebecca and neighbors had converged at my apartment for food and company. As the night wore on, the snow turned to sleet, and Rebecca was beginning to worry about getting back to campus. She asked to take my car, and I said yes, but please, I stressed, go slow. Really. Thirty miles an hour. An hour later the phone rang; it was Rebecca. She had been in an accident; the car had slipped and swerved into a telephone pole. "What happened to the car?" I fumed. "How fast were you going?" Rebecca was silent, then answered slowly, "Not fast," and hung up, utterly dejected. Then she called her mother. "Are you all right?" was all Linette wanted to know. And when Rebecca told her what I had said, her mother explained she knew I wouldn't have responded in such a way if I had not been sure she was okay to begin with.

Rebecca has since said that that night she trembled so hard and cried so long that her pillow was soaked from one side to the other. My reaction to her accident had sucker-punched her—it was a test that I had failed in the extreme. It was not the response of a mother, of that she was convinced, and it had never been so ruthlessly clear. I explained I assumed she was unhurt, otherwise she would've said something right off. But in a way I knew she was right.

28

I could be hard on Rebecca. If I couldn't have a mother, then I could be the mother I did not have, and make a mother-daughter relationship of the ilk I coveted. But I needed her cooperation for that. I wanted her to be as unflawed as I tried to be, and as great as my mother could have been (if she hadn't gone crazy). I wanted to make the most out of a faltering line of females—there wasn't much time. I wanted to correct, with a vengeance, a weak link in our genealogy and to extend into the next generation the best of what my mother and I had shared.

In my constant search for words that would invoke touchstones, a common dream or goal, I encountered sadness and regret time after time, and brought unnecessary pressure to bear on my daughter, who had no way of knowing how to fulfill my wishes about family. Her ideas were so different.

My view of family was created in part from my earliest experience within my home of four, and in reaction to it. Our regimen of daily chores nurtured a self-reliance in my brother and me that I feel lucky to have; my father's make-believe characters added color and made us exclusive members of the same imagination; my mother's deliberate encouragement to question helped us really think about what we thought, so we were trained to know our minds, if not altogether our hearts.

She groomed our critical eyes; we were discerning observers at an early age. Above all, we were expected to earn our floor space, participate, engage. Bottom line: Don't be rude, and contribute.

Over the years I have come to realize that, for me, there are few issues that are more inherently moral than child raising. I can be, like my mother was in her early years, haughty, righteous even, about what is arguably right and wrong about bringing up kids. When we agree to have children, we are bequeathed a consuming responsibility—the ultimate care of another human being. It is a job like no other, unique in its expectations both proscribed and required. If we are good parents, it doesn't much matter—and there are as many good ways of parenting as there are kinds of people; but if we mess up, our children risk being defined by our errors—parents have that power—and are often burdened with the task of undoing the damage long into adulthood. It is humbling, daunting work.

Rebecca's family focused on faith and acceptance instead of expectations, of which there seemed to be few. The hope was that the children would do as they wished, on their own, unencumbered by parental interference or nudging. If their children fell short or were detoured on the way, the Farrells assumed in time an organic resurrection of a clearer course. Rebecca's family grew out of the sixties, when young parents revolted against the rigid head-of-household hierarchies in which they had been ordered around and not listened to. When the closely managed kids of the fifties had kids, they remembered their childhood invisibility all too well and thus granted their offspring a breadth of expression unimaginable in previous eras. "Whatever," parents would say when their unauthorized kids didn't want to clean their rooms or spoke disrespectfully to a relative. Being who you are is quite enough. And being Rebecca, the message seemed to be, was a privilege.

A few years ago, during one of Rebecca's and my bitter breaks, I wrote to her parents, expressing a need to know more about their daughter, an understanding so long overdue. What can you tell me about her as a child? Is it me, or does she ask the world of us all? Rebecca's father wrote back that his kind of parenting differed from mine; he did not subscribe to the "teacher/disciplinarian" role. And Linette wrote that some of the best advice she ever got was from a friend who told her, "Leave the kid alone," when Linette was going through a rough time with her fourteen-year-old son. Linette was suggesting that I take this approach with their daughter; back off, she seemed to be saying, let her be. I wrote back that as a kid who had been left very much alone, I had gotten into some lamentable, foolish trouble, and that I couldn't understand how a child could benefit from parental laissez-faire. I could not feign disinterest—that was not what I felt; more important, I knew Rebecca wouldn't stand for it.

Our brief correspondence became a genial airing of an evident impasse; so opposite were our views that we ended the exchange and have barely spoken since.

I tried to bridge the familial gap between Rebecca and me. I used myself as a reference point of how she should be. At her age, I wanted to know all about my mother, her history, and Rebecca didn't seem to care about mine, or my mother's, even though they shared the experience of adoption. I wanted her to want to know about me; I had tried so hard to figure her out. That way, at least, our differences would sprout from a common well—our shared knowledge of each other. But she was indifferent to my stories, always rerouting our talk when it diverged too far from her, or the mystical story of us.

I continued to set up some common ground rules, a goal-post, a trail of bottom lines, to try to design an environment for two in which I could be something of a parent to my girl. But Rebecca rejected the rules. The alternative was to exit maternal responsibility altogether and simply accept her as another's daughter, at a distance; but that would have been a bitter replay neither of us was ready to bear. Whatever the choice, I could not, I knew, get there without insinuating another kind of rejection.

Yet she pleaded for a daughter's place in my life. Thus began, in her nineteenth year, a torturous no-win balancing act: to spare Rebecca further rejection, to honor her parents and their kind of nurturing, to temper my own restless guilt, and to mother another's child. All this, while I searched for a comfort zone for my own first-time motherhood.

29

For the next few years, Rebecca and I fought. She was approaching adulthood and didn't seem, in the long run, to be absorbing anything I was teaching. When I was not working overtime to soothe or explain, I was demanding, critical, dedicated to her accountability. It was enough to try a good mother's patience to have a child so demanding, yet so unresponsive. But it was a high-grade challenge to accept the reasons for it; she was in every sense but the biological *not* my child. Every clash that interfered with our natural intimacy reminded me I had lost her. And it was not her fault.

Rebecca has said that her mother told her that for a month after her adoption Rebecca was inconsolable. She cried and rejected the comfort she was given. Clearly, Linette has said, her newly adopted baby had undergone a terrible trauma. Instead of celebrating her new family member, Linette was quickly and deeply struck with guilt and sad frustration for her part in separating this baby from her mother. Rebecca's new mother had tried to please her daughter at every turn and vowed, during the first trying months, to keep her daughter happy at any cost. The Farrells' two other sweet-natured (birth) children, ages three and four, would learn to share their parents' considerable attention with their new sister, with the understanding that the new baby needed more of it, given her despondence. She had, after all, suffered an especially jarring start and craved reassurance.

Once, while I was speculating with Merrill about Rebecca's early years, Merrill asked, "Do you know about the cowbird?"

No, I said, I didn't.

"It's an opportunistic parasite. That's not a value judgment, that's what it's called in Peterson's [*Field Guide to the Birds*]. A cowbird doesn't raise its own young. It lays its egg in the nest of another species, making room by removing one of the host's eggs. When the egg hatches, the mother cowbird takes off. The host bird then becomes mother to them all, feeding the baby cowbird as if it were her own. The young cowbird is usually so much larger than the babies of its foster parents and requires so much more feeding that the other nestlings either starve or are crowded out. Is Linette a perfect host bird or what?"

The metaphor made sense. In my experience, some adoptees seem to react to their biological severance by overasserting themselves into the lives of others because, it seems, if they don't they feel they'll disappear. They often see reflections where they do not exist. In effect, they feel the need to be omnipresent, front and center. To relax one's drive to be central is to tempt the overriding fear of flying off forever, unanchored, without a trace. For the surrendered, the absence of grounding can yield a consuming need to create it, always and everywhere.

Thus began Rebecca's reign in her family's house. Her sister and brother stepped aside; the Farrells' adoptee toddled onto center stage, where the spotlight became second nature and her wishes became everyone's concern. When she came to me, I became convinced I could not give her anything because, it seemed, I already owed it to her.

Rebecca's self-perception of specialness, I found out much later, is not uncommon among adoptees. Making their adopted children feel exceptional, or chosen, is one way adoptive parents deal (or don't deal) with their acquired offsprings' feelings of rejection. But it is the first deceit of the legal and social story of adoption. The second is a denial of their adopted children's difference.

Truth telling in adoption is the key to surviving it. Adoptive parents should know from the start that they receive children of trauma—their children's sense of abandonment and the inculcation of their rejection are often nonnegotiable and lifelong. But, like most new mothers and fathers, adopting parents are inflated with naive conceits about the omnipotent effects of their nurturing powers; their love and affection will, they believe, dwarf whatever doubts their children may have about having been left, and good schooling and cultural stimuli will overcome imperfect heredity. They believe their children's lives begin the day they sign adoption papers, the minute they hold them for the first time. In the nurture versus nature debate, the nurture proponents have lofty support in adoptive parents, who for their own purposes, and for the sake of their children, must believe to the end in their ability to nourish and repair, with love, whatever trials their adoptees have suffered or will suffer. Unwavering nurturance becomes an essential factor in bringing up someone else's child, whose genetic history is often a mystery.

Naturally, and with love, adoptive parents often feel the need to shield their adopted children from the fact of their relinquishment, instead of confronting it, explaining it, and then living with it. Some adoptive parents contrive fables, which obscure their children's earthly biological beginnings.

With the vigor of inspired poets, they compose existential tales of free spirits, in the form of motherless babies, landing in their laps, appearing in their homes, and taking hold of their hearts. In these myths, the adopting meant-to-be parents and adoptees become painlessly grafted to each other in familial bliss. In an ideal world, this would be so. How easily families could become.

Some adoptive parents need to believe that they were destined to embrace these wafting orphans from the start, and that somebody else's pregnancy and childbearing were only a shadowy irrelevancy. These survival fantasies are creative medicine for the job of bringing up an abandoned child, and sometimes serve to soothe a woman's aching inability to produce a child of her own. But often the adopted child pays for the pretense; denial and repression of real history can feel like another rejection of the adopted child's authenticity.

I have heard stories about the full-throttle efforts of parents to convince their adopted children that being selected by one's parents is far better than being the take-what-you-get natural-born kind of family member. But being handled with such nervous care can burden any child, and she can feel like a fraud if she fails to measure up. It is a furious dance that requires a constant ovation. In addition, the adoptee is trained to believe that true love entails constant recanting of her specialness and begins to require an exhaustive supply of positive feedback to feel worthy. Who will measure up to the kind of devotion that comes so easily and so consistently? How will the chosen child fare in a world that fails to deliver the accustomed accolades? Mere love pales in comparison.

In our culture, adoptees are called special, chosen, gifts. But if she knows anything, the adoptee knows she has been left, and no amount of high-minded declarations of uniqueness will tranquilize or change that.

A friend once told me that his eleven-year-old adopted daughter angrily declared in the presence of her parents, "You bought me!" My friend, unprepared for such an outburst, pondered this point of view for the first time, and braced for the long melodramatic haul of his daughter's adolescence. I told my friend I thought he must be doing something right, because his daughter's comfort in speaking out invited her family's chance to talk honestly about her surrender and adoption. Now, with increasing public discourse on the subject, at least adoptees will have a forum for what has been for so long secret, troubled questions.

After she turned twenty and was completing her second year of college, I began to talk straight with Rebecca. Over the past two years, I had grown closer with the man who, in her mind, had replaced her; I was distracted by graduate work, two part-time jobs, and the intensifying demands of being the only parent of two preteen boys. I did not have the time or inclination to continue a delicate navigation of her needs. I had not succeeded in easing her melancholy, her constant starvation; and my insistently expressed concern for her lack of caring for those around her was not moving her in the least. I was exhausted and needed to rechart the course, get some perspective. I deferred to the deepest honesty I could find.

I have told Rebecca, yes, I gave you away, but I did not give *you* away. I did not see who you were and then decide I didn't want what I saw. When I was seventeen I gave a baby away because I was still a kid myself. I have said, You were born because of a young girl's off-balance search for her mother's love. You were the innocent part of an error. You did not cause my problem, you did not make it worse. You emerged, beautifully whole, from the fog of my desperate mistake. And I know, no amount of sorries can bring back your wanted beginning.

But no amount of exceptional treatment will help you grow. Nine years after we had met again, Rebecca was a chronological adult, and I thought she ought to begin that growth.

I wrote to her:

July 15, 1989

Dear Rebecca,

. . . I did not choose you. You were born to me, out of my body. I never felt I ought to make you feel special. I have, instinctively, asked of you what I ask of my kids. . . . I know you are fragile about rejection, but I want to give you a chance to be something besides rejected, and I will be damned if I will treat you as a wounded, abandoned baby bird, or a full-plumed peacock for that matter. To me you are another kid. I simply do not know how else to act.

Love,
Jan

30

From a Journal, 1989

Just got a letter from Rebecca in which she declares my
damage to her, again. I am a danger whose prey is this fragile
mocha-girl, whose sweetness and breathtaking beauty are
marred by the boorish reentry of the maker—me—who
walked away. The overbearing, multitendriled, opinion-
spewing plunderer, who shoots truisms like toxic BB's from
the hip into the heart of this exotic orphan.

Page two. Page two. Can we get past this shit? I am
shoveling gelatinous loads of pablum into a raw, gaping girl
and still she is shriveling from emptiness. I am sick to death
of writing white sentences on the chalkboard of my mind
after school: "I am ashamed and I will pay. I am ashamed
and I will pay. . . ."

I am the Return of the Screwed-up Teenager who made
a baby by mistake, slithering slime-covered out of a lagoon to
wreak havoc, again. Just when you, the adoptive mother,
thought it was safe to call her your own. . . .

I am an encore mother, who missed the first eleven curtain
calls. I am an indefensible villain, or a hero whose mere voice
calls up armies of hope and never delivers. I am not mortal,
to this girl. I am never, ever human.

I don't want to be responsible for everyone's feelings within a fifty-mile radius or to exhume buried anger or hidden doubts. I do not want to straighten out anything or anyone. I want Rebecca to grow up, out from under and away from me. And then come back and hold *me*.

Damn it, Rebecca, I cannot grunt you into the world, again.

It has occurred to me: No amount of philosophy, ideology, understanding, analysis, reasoning, perspective, retrospection, introspection, insight, hindsight, theorizing, accommodating, comforting, or invention can get close to the abyss at her center. My words don't soothe, lessen, undo, or correct anything. My letters, presents, hugs, double-chocolate brownies barely skim the wound of her adoption. I want to say: Let it go. Because I can't do this. I can't fix it.

These are labor pains, all over again.

31

What Rebecca and I could not or did not say to each other, we wrote in letters. We carried more words than mere dialogue could contain; we spilled our pain and confusion onto the pages of an arrogant, loving, enraged correspondence, emotionally dueling, baiting and then withdrawing. We wrote ourselves into resignation, when we knew the words didn't matter anymore, when whatever we wrote or said couldn't begin to fill the gulf between us, when we had nothing left to lose.

August 11, 1989

Jan,

Nobody told you that babies were supposed to cry when they're hungry, when they need their diapers changed, or when they need to be held? How much thought did you put into it? Really? I realize that the majority ruled against keeping me, and that you were young and scared, but I find it hard to believe that with your Girls' Latin School intelligence you didn't know that babies cried.

You said to me once, or maybe twice, that you would listen to whatever I had to say as long as there was no meanness. Well, I'm sorry. I feel mean.

My feelings are hurt for lots of reasons. For one, I can't believe I haven't heard from you since our visit. The kids are home, you're probably busy, but how about checking in on me? I feel incredibly vulnerable and defenseless. [We are] The Powerful and The Powerless.

My 19th birthday card from you "Only that I could have held you so much longer," and other times you have distantly expressed a desire to have kept me . . . what are you trying to do? Do you want me to wish that you kept me? Do you want me to hurt for you? You gave me up for adoption, you gave me away. You need to come to terms with your decision. . . .

I have parents and I love them very much. You carried me for nine months, you felt my first breath—without you, I would not be here. I love you more than anyone or anything in this world for that. I loved you that much before I met you. It wasn't until I met you that the resentment set in, seeing your graceful and strong arms that didn't hold me for so much longer.

My mother who raised me said that she hoped my meeting you would add another dimension to my life, and it has. It has also added a lot of hurt and anger and confusion. I wouldn't trade the last nine years of knowing you for anything, but I need your help to put it in perspective.

Much of who I am has been influenced by you. However, not only are D and L legally my parents, but they are also the ones who say, "We love you," and "You look beautiful," all the time. They love me unconditionally. You can't, or won't, or don't—because there's too much pain, or too much at stake. I'm through wishing that you could do the impossible or that I could do the impossible. It just hurts too much, physically.

Love,
Rebecca

August 16, 1989

Rebecca,

Your letter, I confess, surprised me. I had no idea that you felt abandoned (again), or that you were angry. My thoughts have been with you, truly.

. . . It is disturbing for me to have you rate my reasons for and feelings about a very difficult time in my life.

I have felt many things about giving you up. It is a circumstance that is uniquely ambivalent. There are no definite, that's-the-way-it-is ideas about this. I can only suggest that you try and tolerate the ambiguities, to live with the wavering grays. Because adult life, as you must be learning, is slathered with them. When I tell you such things, I do not want you to feel one way or the other. I want you to hear me, and then decide for yourself how you feel. I have no plan.

Comparisons between me and your parents are odious, but, I fear, inevitable. I have known always that [your parents] have loved you unconditionally. As a parent, I know their love for you. I don't need to tell you that you are incredibly lucky to have them for parents and that your relationship with them is different from my relationship with you. We've been over that, Rebecca, a jillion times. If I were to have what you perceive to be an unconditional love for you, it is very likely that it would not be the same brand that you enjoy from your parents. Your parents and I love our children differently.

I am sorry that you feel powerless. I too feel powerless. I have never been able to love you the right way or enough. Indeed, you ask of me the impossible. You want, I think, for me to love you the way I love [my sons]. And this will never happen. I cannot love a child who has parents the way I love a child who has no parents other than me (and his father). I have come to terms with the adoption. I do feel it was the right thing. But I will never really know. This does not mean I do not have pain.

I do. This does not mean that I don't get confused. I do. But I have chosen to live without regret. A steady diet of what-if's has slayed lesser mortals.

I hope you can come to terms with all this too. I know you will. You *are* bright and beautiful and funny and affectionate and loving. And I do love you very much and you are important to me. I am hoping that the inequities of power between us will even out as you become surer and older. I've always hoped for that.

with love,
Jan

August 19, 1989

Jan,

. . . Forgive me for making you feel as though you must verify your reasons for giving me up, but I am the adoptee here.

. . . I certainly don't mean to make comparisons between you and my parents, anymore. There was a time when comparing was the only way I could make sense. Having grown a bit, I realize there is no need. I know who's who, still working on what's what.

Love,
Rebecca

August 21, 1989

Rebecca,

I find your statement that "after all I am the adoptee" arrogant and irrelevant. Nobody, none of us, has a premium on pain. Your feelings of rejection, while I recognize their validity, do not license you in any special regard. Moreover, it must be time to part with some of this. Sometimes it seems you clutch tenaciously to the syndromes, without daring yourself to grow. It seems you are of an age to begin this development.

Your demanding nature has run me ragged. I cannot dance fast or fancy enough to the tune you play. It is as if you insist on rallies at every event in your life which you deem important, and if the response does not suit you, you stamp your feet and issue warnings of dissatisfaction. Makes me want to turn in my Becky Club membership card. Makes me not want to dance at all.

Yes, it has been trying having you try me. I have realized that over the past few years, I have been trying to be all that I can be to you and have met with little success and even less gratitude. I'm tired.

Love,
Jan

August 24, 1989

Jan,

Round III . . . I think perhaps you may have misinterpreted several things I said in my last letter. First, I do appreciate your honest responses. And my statement about being the adoptee was half in jest, I was exaggerating that fact. I've never said that before, although I've felt it and saying it felt pretty funny—because rarely do I, personally, connect my feelings of anger toward you. I know that much of my feelings of rejection come from the adoptee syndrome (which I feel does, most certainly, give me special regard), but when I get down to my feelings toward you, I feel that they are just Jan and Rebecca feelings. So I wasn't trying to gauge pain or anything else in an arrogant manner—really.

I resent you threatening to hand in your Becky membership card because you don't like the issues we're taking up. It is a total contradiction for you to reprimand me for speaking out and then say you want to pull out of our relationship—and whatever happened to being in for keeps? Furthermore, I am, fairly, well, very young—I am just starting all of this stuff; working out my own values and ethics, getting a grip on my relationships. It is by no means time to part with any of this. What I would like to part with, however, is the inequities, competitiveness, lack of simplicity, and discomfort. These letters and these thoughts are the only ways I know how to transcend the yuckiness. Just loving each other is good, and important, but I don't think just loving each other is the end. I think it will help us get through all the other stuff.

We are both worn out for a little while—we've worn each other out. But I'm not ready to stop. I'm in for keeps.

Love,
Rebecca

August, 1989
Rebecca,

I did not say I wanted to pull out of anything except the Rebecca Club. And you can resent that if you wish.

I certainly wouldn't suggest that you part with stuff that will help in working out what it is you feel you must resolve. But a lot of this stuff is getting recycled without benefit of change.

Love,
Jan

A few days after sending Rebecca that letter, I sent another before waiting to hear from her. I had realized, after an initial forgiving response, that I could not let pass the outbursts of the letter in which she mocked my teenage confusion. I did not want her toying with my trauma. Forgiveness is one thing; license to harm is another. Her tyranny of blame was becoming intolerable.

August 25, 1989

Rebecca,

. . . I do believe we are at a crossroad . . . a significant turn in our relationship. For me that turn came when I received your letter, and I feel both relieved and disturbed. Relieved because I was pushed too far, and many things crystallized for me as a result. Disturbed, because I feel distant from you, in some ways.

You have systematically trashed whatever vulnerabilities I've expressed to you. What I have shared in trust has come back at me, in my face, whether it was when I expressed sadness or when I told you about my feelings at seventeen.

And of course you damned me for not loving you deeply enough or unconditionally, like other people in your life.

I have realized how bullied I've allowed myself to be by you. I have been trying to leap through flaming hoops to validate my love, when none of this should've been asked of me, much less attempted by me. We have found ourselves on a treadmill, replaying tired themes. So it is freeing, for me, to know that this part of our relationship is over. . . . I do not agree that I can help you any more. The work left to be done is your work. I think I would get in the way. I feel you must face much of your confusion on your own (or with the help of an objective third party). The source of the problem (me) cannot assist in the resolution of it. Doesn't mean I'm not available for talk, letters, whatever. But my efforts have been unproductive and redundant.

You are always welcome here, you know that.

Love,
Jan

Sept. 12, 1989

Jan,

I am convinced that every two years or so, over the past decade, we have had these fallings out with unreachable resolutions voiced as the "until-next-time" plug. I know that for years I've been trying to hurt you. Because you are right, I've been trying to be better and bigger my whole life. But I think it began because you said way back, "who I was wasn't good enough" but you didn't really. I held you responsible for my self-hate because you rejected me. But, well, we know the rest.

And then the special this and that urged me on. I have felt my whole life that I've needed to lie to be loved, like I've had to manipulate people into believing I was lovable. I guess I've had to bully people into sticking around. [I've] realized how much you've tried to help me (contrary to my belief)—and how I've been trying so hard to get you to love me that I miss it when you do—all the time. It really is time to part with some stuff, and it has to do with your patience and confidence in us (I feel like I'm accepting an Oscar).

Love,
Rebecca

Sept 15, 1989

Rebecca,

I think it is true: that you have been trying to hurt me (and you know I've expected this). But more than that you have been trying to hurt yourself. Consider the persuasive job you've done of convincing me and you that I have not loved you. . . . But, I have loved you all along.

Perhaps you want me to make up for giving you up. It is such useless, dead work. I gave you away. I was unfit at seventeen to be your parent. That was then. This is now. And now is where we must begin. You were right when you wrote a couple of letters ago that you were asking me to be accountable for what I was already accountable for: being me. I think that's what you meant. Maybe you're getting it too.

Love,
Jan

Several letters and a year later, in the fall of 1990, Rebecca and I were estranged. I had said the wrong thing, again, and we had not seen each other or spoken on the phone for nearly eight months. We stopped writing letters. I knew she was at school; she knew I was planning on moving. When I had a new address, I wrote her a letter that began,

There is something oddly familiar about our being apart . . . comfortable, even. Perhaps being separated, yearning, quietly, from time to time for each other is our natural state.

Then I wrote that our house was roomy, her brothers loved their new school, and life was good.

In the meantime, I am not sure what you want from me. You could say I've never been sure. In many ways, in most, I have taken on a responsive role, by providing what (I thought anyway) you've requested, required, or expected. This comes from a fundamental belief that adult needs defer to children's needs. And also from your insistent nature and from my motherly one. That status, of course, has shifted with us over the past couple of years, and it has been a bumpy transition. You have been displeased with me.

Anyway, enough of this. Time and distance and thought are all very good for situations like ours. (Are there situations like ours?)

Rebecca wrote back, seething. How could I be happy without *her*?

Oct. 10, 1990

Dear Jan,

I wouldn't say comfortable, oddly familiar, yes, but comfortable is pushing it. And certainly we yearn for what could've been, but we yearn for each other more than I think either of us realizes.

Sounds as though you are living the high life . . . perfect house, perfect job, perfect kids—jesus I don't suppose anything could be better. . . . [Making more money] should help considerably in maintaining this new sort of lifestyle that leaves little evidence of ever having been a single parent living in low-income housing.

. . . I sure can't figure you, Jan. All I can really seem to figure is that you have been hypocritical during the ten years I have known you. I don't really want much from you, except for you to try to not manipulate the power that you have over me. And as far as letting go of the possibility of being your child—forget it. I am your child. Always will be. While you may feel good about letting me grow, I don't feel as though you are letting me grow, into me, that is. But that is really fine now, because even though it's too late for you to change, it's just in time for me to change. And it's probably better, or maybe even comfortable for me to do it without you, since I started that way.

It all comes down to what I have suspected during the entire ten years we have known each other—if we met on the street, we probably wouldn't like each other much. Fact is, we met at birth, and we can deal with it or not. You keep being you, and I'll start being me, and we'll see how far we get. Perhaps we should start thinking compromise.

>Give my love to everyone.
>
>Love,
>
>Rebecca

By this time, my older son had turned eleven, the age Rebecca was when she came into my life. For the first time, I had a chance to observe the differences between a child I had brought up from birth and the child I had not raised. When my sons were younger, I had no comparable evidence with which to weigh what kind of effect my mothering might have. I always wanted to know what part of Rebecca's behavior was unique to her age, gender, personality, upbringing, and circumstance. Was I expecting too much, or not enough?

When my sons reached their preteens, I observed the similarities of the age in them all—an adolescent self-centeredness, ambivalent resistance to authority, the tyranny of peer acceptance. I observed what I thought to be a striking contrast between my birthchild and my kept children: Rebecca's lack of true empathy. Even in preadolescence, I saw fleeting moments of kindness in my sons, when they were transported, wholly if briefly, into another's experience: when they were around younger children; or when they'd nervously comfort and sit by me when I was sick, or ask worried questions about a neighbor's accident. I do not think they were exceptional in their degree of caring at this age.

When Rebecca and I had each other, during my single-parent years, I felt the generosity I believe belongs to her true self. When she was getting what she wanted—unobstructed access to her original mother—her natural empathy bloomed. But without a vested interest, Rebecca did not seem, even at age twenty, to be able to leave herself, her experience, long enough to join another's. She could not seem to see my life beyond her part in it.

But then, maybe I could not see her life beyond my absence in it? If I had brought her up, I reasoned, my early influence would have adjusted all of what I found irritatingly alien about her. Surely what was missing in this girl was me.

And still I wondered, maybe our dogged alliance was inherent to the ruthless commonality of our gender. Because she was female, did she feel the burden of my yearning, both personal and political, for her to be a better brand of woman, new and empowered, perfect this time around? Did having sons free me from an obligation to improve their lot and free them from my ambitious personal hope? If my kept children were daughters, would we have battled too? Is this what daughters and mothers do—when the mother stays?

And maybe, just maybe, Rebecca never really wanted *me* back. Maybe she came to get what she thought I would give: an identity, an explanation that would soothe the rejection and magically retrieve the vanished years. Maybe to her I would always be an Imagined Mother, not a real woman whose imperfections betrayed her longing for a godly cure to her hurt.

Rebecca's pushing had locked into high gear. Her letter seemed to be inviting a final, guaranteed severance. She mentioned compromise, but it was clear she did not want me happy if my happiness did not involve her. I debated the merit of taking the bait or, against my most visceral urges, coming back with calm conciliation, refusing to draw swords, defiantly maternal.

At the peak of our anger, it seemed neither of us could hear the other past the high pitch of our respective pleas, charges, and countercharges. I had more questions than answers, but far less time and energy than pure instinct. When it was time to move ahead, I leaned heavily on what I felt. This was not working. *At all.*

Oct. 15, 1990

Rebecca,

I cannot be involved in this. I'd like to feel as though I have given you space for the anger which seems inevitable in a relationship such as ours, so I have tolerated a fair amount to date. But I have had it.

Your letter is full of shit. You do not know who I am—from your ill-perceived judgment of my relationship, to the last letter, in which you accuse me of insensitivity to poor people.

In the past year-plus you have deliberately and consistently attempted to hurt my feelings, and hurt they've been. The way you have flung my words back at me is hideous and, in the long run, inalterably damaging to us.

If you let me be happy, you say, then I will forget about the sadness? I've just about had it with your pain, sorrow, and sadness. I will never forget *my* pain, and it's not up to you to let me remember it.

Finally, what stays with me is your lack of understanding about me. I keep thinking something is twisting your perceptions, or that I must have said or done something that you misinterpreted. Then I stop thinking, and simply resolve that it doesn't matter.

I stand by all of the mothering I brought your way. Every single lesson-filled, nagging, insight-packed, opinionated word of it. No regrets. Except, maybe, one. I'm not sure about open adoption. I am seriously very unsure about this.

Jan

I had never before admitted to Rebecca my ambivalence about our reunion. Though I had rarely doubted the value of our eventual meeting, in truth, I had often questioned the wisdom of adolescent adoptees reuniting with their birthrelations. Because Rebecca came into my life at the awkward age of eleven, she did not have the tools to balance and sort out all the information and the barrage of moods that came not only with our strange reconciliation but with her pubescent years, when identity is such a pressing confusion. She was more reckless in establishing her ground with me than a twenty-year-old might have allowed herself to be.

Though I knew it was a harsh disclosure, I could not suffer more of this maligned child, and, besides, I had tried everything else.

Rebecca called a few months later. She said she had spent the weekend reading over our letters—all of them—and she wanted me to know that, despite my criticisms of her, she believed I had always tried to do the right thing. I stayed silent, for once, on the other end of the phone. We made plans for a Christmas visit, and eased back into each other's lives, again.

For the first holiday since we had met, I had no gift for her. She had a card for me. Inside she had written:

> *I heard a woman laugh yesterday*
> *Almost your laugh*
> *It shook me up*
> *Heart and blood*
> *Nothing has warmed me in so long*
> *Not Blankets,*
> > *Not Kisses,*

As that brief stirring moment
Of believing you were near.

I love you.
Rebecca

With these words, my daughter spoke the vexing language that is ours alone. Our nearness to each other could feel like the first and last desperate minute together, over and over again. I looked up and thanked her, tugged off-center by her written words.

Our mother-daughter waltz staggered, soared, and tumbled, in perpetual, agonizing search of a danceable rhythm. She was my unfinished daughter, I was her unreachable mother. In our letters, our plea resonated: We wanted, at least, to be known by each other, the way mothers and daughters know each other, yet we were stung by the impossibility of ever having this.

After our Christmas visit, she wrote and said she felt lonely on holidays without her brothers and wanted to know some of the details surrounding her adoption. I answered, committed to keeping it light, and eased back into being parental.

January 13, 1991

Dear Rebecca,

Great seeing you over the holidays. It seems, sometimes, that we are enmeshed in exercises in exorcising. It seems every patch of time we have together, we unearth yet another pondersome thing to be studied and resolved. Maybe some days we should talk about hard bodies and clothes. . . . About the inconsistencies in data re: adoption signing and such. Your parents, as I've said, would have a better remembrance of this. And as it turns out, I do think I signed the papers more than a year after the fact. I was in college, so it would have had to have been at least in my twentieth year. I put it off, and off. I remember that. And your mother never talked me into the adoption, but I think I said that before. If anything, she tried to talk me out of it.

. . . About holidays etc.: I think the right thing is to be with your parents. I have learned to adjust and keep learning (and sometimes it's hard) to live with the fact that your parents place first with parental rights, and that they justly deserve your presence at family days. Daniel and Linette should not have to make that adjustment. They have made adjustments of the giant kind, adapting to bigger things for the past ten years. I hope you will understand this. If your heart isn't there, that will be tough. But during these occasions maybe your heart isn't the one that counts. Christmas Eve, we know, will always be ours.

Look forward to seeing and talking with you, next week, my dear. The struggles, in all their nagging harmony, continue . . . and will, perhaps, forever. For this we must be prepared.

Love,
Jan

32

I was convinced that Rebecca and I would never have a casual, warmhearted assumption of each other. It was heat or frostbite. Being together was often a merciless tease of what could have been or a panging reminder of what would never be.

There were and still are times when I kiss her up close that her face feels like the baby skin I knew twenty-four years ago and will never forget. All of me dissolves into the moment of touch, as if we are joined by flesh and dew, willingly inseparable. She feels fiercely familiar. Then it is obvious. She is mine. I am hers. I begin to feel an emergency kind of love that I want to rush to her with, before it or she goes away; I am a commuter, panicked, racing in the dark to catch the last train home.

But they were rare moments—when my love for my girl soared. My primary assignment, the one I could know, had always been and would always be the keeper of the deal: the commissioner of the pact that had set my infant free from me. Like a hostage who assumes devotion for her imprisoner, I welcomed the legal guidelines in the otherwise threatening maze that our union had become. I did not want to erase Rebecca's parents or forget their fears: I felt compelled to honor their profound preemption of me—the technical parent, the producer. If I were to dishonor their intimate parenting of the girl I had given them, I would slight my own, which I hold dearly, sacredly close.

But I could not be half a mother, as surely as I could not be a little bit pregnant. For me, I began to know, it was and is a heart-and-soul job, and I could not suspend selective pieces of my motherly ties. I often felt like I was watching Rebecca ready to spring into the road in the path of a speeding car, and I could not make my voice scream for her to stop. Being with Rebecca, as the quasi mother, became as impossible as being without her during the torturous days following her adoption.

Part IV

Staying This Time

33

For the next few months, still sore from our letter pelting, Rebecca and I stayed away from the written word, as if the ink itself would reactivate the chill. The medium was the message—once we reverted to letters, we seemed to know, the spoken word had failed to comfort or explain, yet again.

We had been exercising a tradition of hyperliterariness, writing with an eye to the anthologist. My family could put a word on the page, and we knew it. When my mother became ill, she contrived a voluminous, eerie correspondence with her fabricated enemies; later, when we were estranged, her garbled accusations arrived in the mail to us all. And instead of calling on birthdays, visiting during holidays or after the birth of his first grandchild, my father sent quick notes laced with bons mots and wordplay. When my brother and I were at odds one year, the anger was documented in venomous missives; we referred to the chronicled assaults for months after as proof of our respective derisions. Letter writing had become a run for cover, a cowardly detour into the precise word or well-turned phrase, our easy reserve; it was cleaner than fumbling in the flesh with conflict. We tossed sentences instead. Correspondence, especially after our family was scattered, had not redrawn our intimacy but rather replaced it. And Rebecca could trade words with the best of us.

I grew tired of the vain athletics letter writing had become.

After a year of urgent mail, if we wrote at all we kept it undangerously brief. In the spring of 1991, we met for pizza in Harvard Square instead.

On our way to the kiosk, we began to talk—about us, again. Rebecca had recently spent time with her uncle, my brother, and had understood a few things for the first time. My brother told her that it wasn't so much the lack of money or a place to live, and not necessarily my age; mostly, he said, it was the absence of any emotional support in my life that contributed to my decision to give her up. There was no one there for me. My grandmother was too old, my mother was gone, and while my brother would always be there for me, he had felt powerless to improve or change the situation.

Rebecca had always seen me as a capable adult parent. She could not imagine, she said that evening as we sat on a stone wall in a crowd, knowing me as she does, that I could not have handled a baby, her, when I was seventeen. She never truly had a sense or a full understanding of what it was like for me to have been young, pregnant, poor, and alone; and she said the incidentals—the lack of money, my age—always seemed superficial reasons for the adoption. But when my brother explained the loneliness of my dilemma, that made sense, she said.

"Also, he had no reason to lie. I believed him," Rebecca said. "I thought for the longest time that you might say whatever it took to excuse what you had done. I had relied on people who didn't know or love you like he does to explain what I needed to know." At twenty-one, she finally held glimpses of the picture, at last able to grasp, if fleetingly, the answer to her unyielding question, "Why?"

★ ★ ★

Rebecca's understanding came and went after that night in Cambridge. She could know the story but still felt bitter about it. I made an appointment for us with a psychologist who specialized in adoption. For all our hard-earned insights, we couldn't seem to sustain peace between us. Rebecca canceled. I went anyway.

One of my mistakes in dealing with my daughter the adoptee was in expecting her behavior to coincide with her chronological age, said the psychologist Joyce Maguire Pavao, an adoptee. Adoptees, I was told, often take a long time to grow up, and are often years behind emotionally. Ironically, Rebecca had always been called a precocious, sophisticated girl. My brother saw this in her, her parents marveled at it. But there had been, all along, a lost, much younger girl inside.

Rebecca had grown up in a small, all-white, rural town, and to the people in her community she was a mystery, an exotic (as in not indigenous) puzzle. With such unfamiliar looks and uncertain origins, all of what Rebecca was was called sophisticated, for lack of a better understanding. And Rebecca could pull it off—she was a clear-eyed, pretty child with a convincing smile; she was affectionate, generous, and smart. She was her father's girl à la mode, favored and adored. She walked in the empress's new clothes, when all she was was a young girl trying on faces, acting the parts, looking for her Self—the key to which, she felt, was missing, along with her genetic family.

Rebecca became imprisoned in a role that stuck, and she was afraid to break out and be young. She was besieged by adults eager to prove their worldliness and humanity (who assumed she knew so much more than she could have) and was drawn into their confidences at a young age; she was given gifts of custom-made clothes, silk hats, and jewelry.

Through no fault or contrivance of her own, Rebecca became a child célèbre.

And what's to keep a child from taking on accolades from those around her? A child is not about to level her fans with an insistence on her average youthfulness. The young Rebecca slipped unwittingly into the place prescribed for her and hoped that no one would find out that it was a lie.

What Rebecca needed was a community that was willing to acknowledge her difference without romanticizing it, without declaring that *what* she is—biracial, adopted—is *who* she was.

When she grew tired of holding up her ermine train and began to be eaten up by the fraud of it, she started to shed the imposed persona that had taken her so far into young adulthood. But it was not easy. Defrocking made her feel unusually naked—there was nothing underneath, so she would curl back up under her furs and try again in a moment of strength or unbearable discomfort. She began to realize that the time and energy siphoned to maintain a workable public Rebecca could have been diverted to the work of forming the true one, the second-nature self.

In the sixties, zero population growth was in. Some liberal white families who already had children and wanted more adopted black babies, out of social responsibility, because there were more of them. The result: a generation of culturally white, cosmetically black children often isolated from half their heritage. There was a time, through high school and part of college, that Rebecca was drawn to blond and blue-eyed boys, because that was the ideal with which she had grown up; yet their attentions were rarely available to her, even though she was considered "beautiful." In recent years, she has been hungry to know the biological family whose stories could teach the experience of moving in black skin in this world. I cannot know her black experience. Her adoptive parents cannot help with this. Transracial adoption provides added trials for the adoptee, who lives not in two cultures but is often disqualified by both.

So, in her early twenties, Rebecca was ready to grow herself, but she didn't know how to begin. And all the in-place support an adolescent has (under the best of circumstances) when she is ready to individuate—parents, school, peers in similar struggles—had long since folded up and gone on. Rebecca, who needed help and understanding in order to go on with the work of becoming, found herself feeling not in the least a sophisticated prize. Because when one reaches her twenties, she is no longer a precocious child and is expected to pay her bills, have direction and at least an inkling of a sense of herself. Rebecca, at twenty-two, felt foolishly late and alone.

34

Rebecca could not, her knowledge notwithstanding, integrate her adopted and birthdaughter selves. She would begin to become herself by becoming her parents' daughter and most certainly not mine. This became recognizable in her letters, especially after she had visited her parents.

After I had met with the psychologist, I wrote to Rebecca, explaining certain adoptee phenomena. I was sure she'd want to know. She held me in contempt for the intimacies I dared assume of us. How dare I discuss her life with a stranger? she wrote, as if she were stepping to the far corner of the room, buttoning up her coat, and making clear her imminent exit. She was not mine to care for or worry about, she wanted me to know.

Rebecca had fine-tuned the luxury of turning from one family to the other when she sensed discomfort or disapproval. If the demands of our family pushed her too far, she could phone home to her adoptive parents for reassurance. If her family exasperated her, she could come to us—the birthrelations—to be heard and seek support. She never allowed herself to go up against the wall, or into corners, where she just might find her way out. With such fickle family loyalties, she averted and was therefore denied the chance to know that she could persevere, that she could stay the course and advance, even, into maturity.

When adoptive families are in any way intertwined with birthfamilies, a strong home ground seems essential—a constant, clear assertion of family rules and borders. In most instances, the adoptive family must be the primary family—a beacon of references—in order to provide a secure base of operations for the developing child. In Rebecca's case, the force of family came from outside the borders, leaving her stranded in the middle, never sure where to turn when she needed absolute authority. I had the authority—an emphatic parental nature—without the jurisdiction; her parents had the jurisdiction without presuming their authority.

I needed and wanted more than anything during those trial-and-error years to hear Rebecca's parents' resounding ordinances regarding their daughter's journey with me. I pushed for their intervention, by pointing Rebecca back to them, if only to be free to figure out my part. But doing so backfired often and multiplied our troubles; she took my pushing as pushing away.

After she sent the letter in which she accused me of interfering (because of my visit to the therapist's office), I called Rebecca. I was livid. I told her that her letter reeked of secession—that she was pulling away from the hard work when it could matter. And, I yelled, how dare she accuse me of interference, when that was what she had demanded from the start? She backed down and softly confessed she was tired of struggling with divided loyalties, what we called her double-daughter status. Her love for me meant a betrayal of her parents, and feeling close to them must mean she would have to become less attached to me. She felt, too often, ripped in two.

She manipulated and guarded a growing chasm between me and her parents. The thought of her mother and me in the same room became nightmarishly uncomfortable for her; it would have meant a monstrous clash of Rebecca's two selves, not yet reconciled to comfortable coexistence. She felt impossible, she said, over and over again.

I suggested she consider herself something other than a daughter to me. Think of it this way, I said, in the interest of simplicity (always unreachable but ever aspired to in our circumstance): You are first and foremost your parents' child. We can work on what you are to me, because I can live with whatever adjustments you might need to make it easier for you.

"Do you know how that sounds?" she screamed. "I am your daughter, like it or not." And she hung up.

I hung up. I thought I would collapse from frustration. I felt ill, insanely exhausted.

Enough. To Hell with the mother and daughter whose lives I had tracked and tried to retrieve, with long-winded letters, late-into-the-night talk, and honest-to-God empathy. No more bargaining, no more probing and forgiving the hungry, battered hearts of the wounded adoptees in back and in front of me. No more I-can-so-I-will, doing-the-work-of-the-woman altruism. I wanted an easy family. I had had it with crash-and-burn confrontations, the last-breath intensity of being familial. So my mother and daughter would, once and for all, exit my adult life; it was clear, they could not bear me in theirs.

After years of living with the looming warning of a horrid, final severance, I approached this separation with a sense of relief. My incurable hopes—for big, noisy holidays of happily bumping bodies in a busy kitchen in between vegetables and dirty dishes—had been cured. I would not chase them this time. I'd had enough heart-to-hearts and outed family secrets to last a lifetime. I wanted to talk skin moisturizers and plant bulbs in the dirt on my knees next to my mother; I wanted to have soothing, silent bicycle rides to the beach with my daughter. I had mother-daughtered to death. If all our female relatives could do was wallow in the written passionate word, or exist only in the strenuous moment, I wanted nothing from them at all. But I was shattered too, because my hope for a certain kind of family, a gathering of daughters and mothers, had been revised for the last time.

I went out on the back porch, sat and stared, shooed away the cats, the kids, went limp. I resolved at that moment to stop trying. I wanted out of the corner for the accused into which my daughter's want, my mother's absence, and my yen for deliverance had shoved me.

Since the day we met again, Rebecca had tried to return to my womb in a dozen ways. She had been waiting for a blessed permission to begin, because she loathed so impatiently the beginning she had been given—away from the body where she unfolded, at her own pace, in her own place for the last time. Like the last child left at the day-care center, a sweet-faced remnant full of incorruptible hope, Rebecca will always have a part of her that will be waiting in a darkening room for Mom to pick her up, even though I am here now and will always be, even though Linette would never forget. She will be distracted, rootless, waiting, unsure, and no amount of comfort or explaining will soothe her. *For some adoptees, the search is more for the missed and forever lost mothering than it is for the missing mother.*

Rebecca wrote to me shortly after our phone call and accused me of destroying her. I wrote back:

April 25, 1992

Rebecca,

What in the sweet confounding name of Jesus H. Christ do you want from me?

I said that [you should consider yourself your parents' daughter only] because I felt your torment as I do now and because I thought it would simplify your life, knowing I could and would adjust to almost anything if it would contribute to your comfort. I see you shift back and forth, tossed and torn, and it is agony for me to observe, it must be hell to live it.

I think this is not a good time for us to be talking about these things. I am sorry. I wish I could make it all go away, and give you comfort and peace, or whatever it is you want. I can't. I'll just keep sticking around.

I am destroying you. And you are emotionally dehydrating me. Wonderful.

Good luck with school. I love you, Rebecca Anne Farrell.

Jan

Every year since Rebecca's birth, I had wondered, with waning interest, if I would ever have my mother back. I had considered, with varying degrees of optimism, realism, and resignation, what it might be like. Now, I declared, I just didn't care. There were other people—my sons, my sweetheart, my friends—who wanted and deserved my time.

35

Still, like watching the roof tumble in on a burning home, I felt both desperate to flee and damned to stay—to save the salvageable. Since the day I met Rebecca for the second time, as often as I may have felt resigned to a final severance, I knew I would not leave her. I could not do it again. This time, I thought a hunt for data could take me back to her and keep us together, if not emotionally bound, then joined by facts. Maybe documentation could authenticate an otherwise fuzzy kinship—a legal declaration amid the torrent of guesses and questions, something to hold on to. First I contacted the city hall in the town where Rebecca had been born. There was no birth certificate. "Once the adoption takes place, the original birth record no longer exists," I was told. At the legal moment of adoption, explained the clerk of the court, the birth certificate was "filled out as if her adoptive parents were her parents, y'know, the real parents, the natural ones."

In 1992, court-ordered lies were still responsible for ersatz birth certificates; a biomother and her lost child still must suffer legal humiliation in order to obtain the simple documented truth.

"So in other words, the birth certificate which now exists is false," I said, perturbed.

"Not really," she said.

Then I called the hospital where Rebecca had been born and told a woman in the records department I was looking for the medical file of a baby I had had in 1969 but had subsequently given up for adoption. She put me on hold, then returned to the phone.

"You're sure you delivered here?" she asked. (Did she think that I, the childless mother, was so mentally depraved that I would not remember the place of such a personal event?) She could not locate my medical records or Rebecca's; they were lost or destroyed, she said. I could write to the Bureau of Vital Statistics to request a birth certificate, she suggested.

I called instead. I explained my circumstances—that I was a birthmother looking for the birth record of the baby I had delivered twenty-three years ago.

"Oh, you can't have access to those records. You'll have to petition the court, and then the judge will make up his mind. Even then, the file will not be open to you directly. I'll send the forms."

"But they are my records. I had the baby."

"We don't know the situation."

"I can tell you."

"You'll have to petition the judge."

A few days later the hospital called to say they had found the baby's records, but there was no cross-reference with the mother's file, the usual procedure when a baby is born. The search so far had produced little more than frustration: Rebecca had been born, yes, but there was no evidence that a mother, I, had brought her into existence.

Filling out a lengthy petition (which I would have to have notarized) to gain access secondhand, through the court, to records that were mine and Rebecca's to begin with and having to approach Rebecca's parents for their permission and plead my case to a judge who presumably knew what was best for Rebecca and me, both legal adults, was time-consuming and degrading. Why was I groveling for permission to know what I already knew? The pursuit of information regarding Rebecca's beginning atrophied into resentment, resulting in the opposite of the desired effect—blurred powerlessness—and I abandoned the search for my records. The law says she is another's child. So we go on faith.

After agonizing for years over what seemed like an intangible loss—an instinct-driven motherlove for my daughter—I began to know that the sum of the difference between what I felt for Rebecca and my other children was what I harvested by staying with my sons and what I had lost by leaving my daughter.

But it was the lost years and more that had deadened a motherly pull to her. Rebecca's nature was different from mine, I reasoned; in the intervening years she had become unfamilial to me.

Then I thought, because our natures were so different, a slow, clumsy reconnection would be inevitable. But I am as different, in many ways, from my sons as I am from her; only my ties with my kept children can bear the difference. So much of what is assumed among us—that I will not leave them, that I never have, the in-jokes of our collective genealogy—is vigorously, dangerously, perpetually in question with Rebecca. In the first few years this uneasiness with her was always close to the skin. I carried her heart around like glass blocks in a bag; I knew I could tip her over with the wrong words. So I found myself trying to reinvent her to soften the distress of our alienation; I tried to extract a girl of my own, a recognizable child, someone who could bear the differences.

Slowly, grudgingly, I came to understand that the reasons for our struggle were irrelevant; when I gave up Rebecca, I relinquished the right, the privilege, and the trial of laying the soil in which she would be rooted and bloom. The first decade of our children's lives, it became clear, matters most. After that, parenting is melioration or police work (as a friend calls it), nudging wanderers back into the borders (a process that, in most cases, should be undertaken no less vigilantly than law enforcement). The mental geography, the emotional catalogs, the approved familial routes, and the common language are all firmly established before adolescence; and the more firmly they are set, the easier it is to grow—against or into them. Like a ballerina turning on toe, focusing on an immovable mark to keep vertigo at bay, our kids need the checkpoint of a grounded guardian so they can move—freely, fully—without losing their balance. And if they truly know themselves, with the help of our thoughtfully placed mirrors, they can take it on the road, anywhere, with anyone, at home in their skin, at ease in their world.

I know no matter how obnoxious or frustrating my sons can be, I can meet them on some common plane. I can invoke a mutual moment. I feel I can always reach them— though sometimes not until hours of silence or anger later. I did not have that internal assurance with my birthdaughter. We had not been family, and my words fell flat or far away too often. Rebecca, dizzy from unfocused origin, had neither a firm imprint nor the chance to get one by the time she met me, and when I gave her away I lost the right to offer mine.

36

When I first told Rebecca that I was sorry, when I was thirty-nine and she twenty-two, we were in my car, parked in the rain, waiting for her car to be fixed in a nearby garage. I cannot remember what we were talking about, but I felt a surge of remorse that I finally was able and desperately wanted to express. I looked at my grown-up girl and wanted to tell her for the first time how much I hurt for her. Like a case of violent hiccups, the spoken words triggered an unstoppable rush of "I'm sorrys." I cried and apologized, turned away into my tears, and apologized more. My daughter, silent, wet-eyed, placed her hand on a rueful mother's arm, and said, "I know." Eleven years after we reunited, when I had known her as many years as I had been without her, Rebecca and I began to know each other for the first time. Emerging from the fog of our grief and blame, we were listening, at last. For once, she was the consoler, I was the comforted, and we had vaulted yet another shaky hurdle on the road to reunion.

I had hauled around guilty remorse since the day I had given Simone away, but I had dodged, explained, tried to adjust or fix her hurt while we were together. I would not say I was sorry for my decision to give her up, because I could never know whether her adoption was the wrong choice. But, I finally realized, I could be sorry for the pain the adop-

tion had caused her without accepting blame for a bad decision. When I was finally ready, the spoken words felt like a
declaration of independence from being harnessed by my
errors and her accusations. My deep-felt recognition of her
hurt announced the end of my allegiance to it.

Months later, Rebecca met me after work. We walked to my
car and sat. (We often met in cars like hungry lovers, trading
hot talk and stolen time.) Eventually she turned the talk to us.
I was visibly less willing than she to embark on the topic. She
had been hurt, she said, by something I said. I did not ask
what it was that she had objected to but simply stated that I
thought she might, for once, consider how I may have felt.
"It is time," I said, "for you to think about what others feel."

"I'm working on it," she said, referring to the eternal hunt
for self-realization.

I looked gravely into her brown eyes and declared, "I'm
not." I resisted the details, the usual investigation of her
discomfort. I was retiring from the labor-intensive phases of
our union. Done. Though she looked surprised, she did not
fight me. She seemed to believe it and said, "Okay."

I told Rebecca the romance didn't work for me anymore.
I didn't want to waste any more time on what-ifs, or lapse
into sentimental sadness about our drama. I am forty, I told
her, and feel mortal, and there just isn't enough time for this
psychic deconstruction, the charges, the doom, the pathetic
disenchantment of suffering adoptees and runaway mothers.
I told her I had forgiven myself, even if she hadn't.

A few days later I had a dream about Rebecca. In the dream
we had been apart for what seemed months, a self-imposed
exile from each other, choosing, again, the lesser ache of
estrangement over the agitation of each other's company.

When I finally saw Rebecca, in a pall of sadness, she was pale, not white, but her skin had faded into a translucent beige. She was much calmer, at ease, but she was somber, as if she had accepted that the price of her peace was sorrow.

I missed her, wanted to hug her, but didn't, and stayed distant because of an understanding. We seemed paralyzed by our surrender to the inevitable, and then she vanished and I was alone.

37

Rebecca's birthbrothers, my sons, have always treated her with unusual care; they are proud of her in the way young kids beam at siblings who are older but have not yet crossed over to dull adulthood. Whenever Rebecca visited, my younger son would take out the photo albums with the pictures of her, and she would feel included. Her brothers have never felt threatened by or jealous of their sister; they have, on the contrary, always felt protective of her, somehow understanding that they have what she was denied—me. When Rebecca and I have disagreed, they have tried to explain her to me, and me to her. They are deeply, generously loyal to us both.

Over the years, my sons have asked me if I ever regret my decision to give away Rebecca. Their asking is both protective and vulnerable; they don't seem to want to believe that their mother could be capable of giving away a baby, and their sister's sense of rejection has always been palpable to them. I think they want me to say, "Of course. If I had it to do all over again, I would never part with a child of mine." My younger son always answers the question himself: "You should've kept her, Mum." Sometimes I explain by saying, "I have no regrets, though I'm sorry she hurts. But if Rebecca hadn't been adopted, you would not be here, and, God, I can't even begin to think about that."

But none of us, my sons and I, can imagine our world without her. In the end, a policy statement is an imperfect translation of the experience. Ultimately, there is no answer.

Until recently, there were many taboos in the language Rebecca and I shared. For the first ten years I could not say to her, for instance, what I guilelessly said to my sons when they interrupted or were being bothersome: "That's nice. I love you. Go away." Or when one of my sons was complaining about sibling inequity, I would kid, "It's because your brother is better and I prefer him."

"Funny, Mum," my kids would say with a droll smirk, as they walked out of the room, as unserious as I. So assumed is our pliant relationship that questioning it becomes a goof. But the words I spoke to my sons would have taken on new meaning if I had said them to my birthdaughter. To tell her to go away would have been fearfully close to our first shared trauma, and to declare, even in jest, my preference for another child, whom I had kept, over her, whom I had not, would have been cruel.

One day after Rebecca, my sons, and I had finished supper, I asked my older son to do the dishes. He began insistently claiming that I liked his brother better because he, the older, had been asked to do the dishes twice in a row. No question, he argued, the younger, cuter kid was favored. After listening to the righteousness of the wronged adolescent one complaint too many, I said, "Imagine how Beck feels," and my older son grew instantly silent. He looked over at his sister and meekly smiled, and then, as he strolled into the kitchen, we all laughed heartily, to the point, almost, of tears.

38

It has occurred to me that the most regrettable part of my years of growing into a woman was never having made a choice. When young, again and again I chose not to choose at times when a decision was not only important but imperative. I floundered in limbo, aggressively passive, willing to have results fall on me when I might have changed experiences that could and *did* alter my life forever.

I decided to have sex (though it was his idea and I relented), but I did not decide to have sex without contraception; I simply chose not to think of pregnancy as a consequence of unprotected sex. I did not choose a full-term pregnancy; I merely slipped into unconsciousness during the months when the decision could have been made to terminate it safely. I did not choose to give away my baby; I withdrew, deferring to the voices around me. I shrank from considering the outcomes I could have affected and surrendered my sense of self-preservation, willing to defer to disinterested fate. I did not want and was not ready for responsibility, so I let it go and waited defiantly—and futilely—for my mother to retrieve it.

As I drill my teenagers on the responsibilities before them, I am reminded that I backed down before or snuck away from seeing the choices before me. Look at it this way, I say to them when they are confronted with the dangers of their age, you have choices: Consider seriously the right one, it is yours to make.

39

When my father died in 1993, I wrote to my mother for the first time in over five years and let her know. My letter was a short, sad announcement, an affectionate homage to his grace during the final days of his life. She wrote back, obviously touched, with warmth and lucid regret. She said that she had never stopped loving him, that my brother and I ought to feel proud of the way we'd handled a difficult time, and that she would write again, when the shock had worn off.

During this time I had also written her that I had found her birthmother. Did she want to know more? Did she want to meet her? Yes, she wrote, tell me all. But no, after all these years without a mother, she was almost certain she didn't want one now.

I allowed myself fleeting visions of an in-the-flesh reunion. But after less than a month of letters both senseless and thoughtful, her words turned vicious; she had, again, lapsed into paranoid accusations. My mother had come perilously close to the terrain of her emotions, dabbled, even, in intimacy. And for the adoptee closeness is not closeness alone; it is packaged inseparably with severance, and severance is intolerable. Our brief correspondence had become a scary encounter, a horrible soreness, and again she had retreated. I stopped writing. A month passed before my mother wrote, declaring she did not want to "break the thread completely." She finally agreed to see me.

After a ten-year separation, my mother and I met for lunch.

As we walked the streets of the city, I noticed, when I could, that her face had more lines, her voice had weakened with age, and she moved more slowly than when I had seen her last. But she was familiar within minutes. Our reunion was easier than we had imagined. It was as if no time had passed, she said, both amazed and grateful.

But she was seeking acquittal. She wanted to clear things up at once and began explaining a half dozen times. "It has occurred to me that you must be angry, or you must think I feel guilty. I don't. I feel badly. But there was nothing I could do," she said, referring vaguely to hostile forces that had taken hold of her family. Back then, she said, she felt as if her life had become meaningless. "I felt so awfully isolated. I was losing [my husband], everything," she said, on the edge of tears.

I said that now I am not angry, though I was (hence the pregnancy and bad-tempered men), but that I knew she could not help what had happened—only I was talking about her emotional collapse. We talked it out—she with her own references, me with mine—and we were able to stay with each other, sustained by our separate versions, meeting in the middle of the bigger truth: that her absence and our family's demise were beyond her control. Together over quiche and coffee, we absolved her of blame.

"I never knew how much you and [your brother] were a part of this," she said cautiously.

"We would never be a part of anything that would cause you pain. You have to believe that. But if you don't, then we'll have to agree to disagree."

"I'm glad to hear that," she said, perhaps less than convinced in her own mind, but at least willing to suspend her suspicions for the day.

I was comforted to see my mother, but I knew before I saw her that I had no yen to brandish the happiness I had found, though she asked and I gladly talked. Her responses were important, but not crucial in the way a mother's words can be. Her interpretations used to cut me; I used to keep an active tally of her approvals and disapprovals that stuck to my heart and crippled my instincts.

Before I met her again, first against my will and then naturally, I had shed my daughterhood and all that it entailed. I always missed having a mother, but I needed her less each year she was out of reach. And she too must have known—from my letters—that what little I was asking after all this time she might be able to provide. Years before she could not help but feel my requests for the kind of mother she could not be; it must have pained her to fall so short of a growing daughter's need. During our reunion, my mother seemed relieved to know that her petitioning child had finally retreated and that an independent woman had emerged.

After I saw her, I felt so free from the motherjudge within that I was ready to recommend an extended estrangement as a cure to my adult friends who are still so afflicted by their critical mothers. There are few daughters who do not know that disconnecting emotionally from our mothers is hard work, and I began to think I had been given a circumstantial leg up. I had been forced by the events in my life to see myself as separate, and in the intervening years I had become my own mother. So the reappearance of my original one seemed almost extraneous.

Sometimes I am convinced that her absence, during the tough years of self-discovery, was a subconscious stroke of genius. She must have known, instinctually, that she would have been an unbearable interference had she remained a part of my life.

My favorite Doonesbury comic strip, by Garry Trudeau, involves Mrs. Doonesbury explaining to her child's teacher how important girls' self-esteem is. "Those early, empowering influences are so important. In my case," Mrs. Doonesbury says, "I learned from my mother to be tough and independent and stand on my own."

"How'd she teach you?" the teacher asks.

"Well, by . . . um . . . abandoning me. Okay, bad example."

Not necessarily.

The fact is, my early sense of belonging, so fiercely and lovingly provided by my mother, and the independence granted by my father, combined with a compulsory self-reliance in the years following, often feels like the perfect albeit pricey formula for self-actualization. By forty I was blaming no one, and I knew what I could do—which was plenty.

Now, divested of our symbiotic tension, Sara and I met not as a mother and her daughter but as imperfect peers with a history. Before our food arrived, we were finishing each other's sentences. We spoke of people we loved in a language that awakened our common memories. We recalled my father's rare imagination, mourned his death, and cried together amid booths of chattering people.

Sitting across from my mother after years of separation and ruined faith seemed as natural as sharing breakfast with my sons that morning. Having been family from the start seemed to yield an infinite supply of reprieval. And growing up had given me the grace and humility to move ahead.

"I can't believe I have middle-aged kids," my mother sighed as we paid the bill.

"And here we are, you and me, two old ladies," I said.

When we were ready to leave and without thinking, I closed her collar against the cold. Protecting her even now was second nature; it had taken years after my reunion with my daughter to loosen the strain of holding her. On my way home, this bittersweet revelation wouldn't leave me.

I had been estranged from my mother roughly the same number of years I had been missing from my daughter's life. Yet, for my mother and me, it was *as if no time had passed*. For Rebecca and me, it will always feel as if time has escaped. Rootlessness had stolen our faith in forgiveness.

40

Since the beginning of 1993, Rebecca and I have met, as friends and women, over lunch or coffee; she comes for supper and spends the night; we talk on the phone about writing books, movies, cooking, our bodies, movie stars, and men. Sometimes we skip a week or two, using the break to cool off, because we both know when we have come to the edge of an inflammatory letdown. Eventually we forget about it or clear it up. Sometimes I cannot believe I have a daughter; but when I allow myself to, I feel so damned lucky. Our senses of humor have always been similar, but now, as women, what we find funny is identical and nourishes us both. We speak in shorthand, a language tried and stretched that grows by the day. No one gets our words the way we do.

Occasionally we talk about the ironies of us, but I am coming to her on my terms. I realize there's a chance she may never know or love me apart from how I have affected and continue to affect her life. But when I feel she has again failed to see me, I am more patient. I can wait. The years, I know, will give her the sight, as they have me. When I see her, I kiss her and mean it; our hugs are tighter and longer than ever. We have agreed to give up the drama.

I have stopped feeling as if it were my job to make up for the sins and longing of mothers past. I no longer feel I have to be a parent whose every move is rife with conscious generational corrections, to communicate loudly and unmistakably my heart-filled promise to stay. I was often to my birthdaughter what I would have wanted of a mother, but not what she has always needed; I have nurtured her, sometimes, afire with guilt, aggressively penitent, duty bound. And sometimes I have been jealous, because she has had two mothers when I have had none.

My daughter would say that all these years we've been getting back to the business we began twenty-five years ago, on May 19, before that even. But I see it differently. It has taken me as many years living with Rebecca as living without her to figure out that our relationship is a determination *endowed* by our genetic similarities, not *necessitated* by them. When I am not saddened by this, I am relieved to truly know it.

Now I know that I am her mother and she is my daughter because above all else that is what we want; we have lived the alternative, and it is unbearable. We believe in each other like religion. Packing up our losses, we move on.

But for me there will always be a melancholic aftertaste about Rebecca's and my story. It is not so much the haunting what-ifs but the unnaturalness of having a child who is not mine and, for her, having a mother who belongs to someone else. Ours is an adulterous kinship, sans decree, carried out against the wishes and in spite of the fears of a few. Holidays, birthdays, graduations—there are awkward limits to how jubilant and engaged we can become on those days and a million others.

The hardest days are when Rebecca is down—humbled yet again by the tangled paradox of her existence. When she is vulnerable, I can see past her somber eyes into the heart of the kept child—her natural mother's girl. The womanchild revealed is clear-eyed and at rest. Her spirit is supple and unbruised; she has not had to fight the awkward contradiction of growing up as a celebrated member in someone else's family, an absentee in her own. She is the girl she would've become, if only . . . When the vision of my unadopted daughter fades and I am left facing how lost she really feels and how impossible it is for me, or anyone, to fix it *now,* I want to sob and shriek my way back to 1969 and *never* let her go. It is the single most regretful impulse I know.

If my daughter and I sustain our reconnection, it will be because we have cultivated our kinship as captives of a continuous hope for restoration. But there will never be an easy second-nature pull between the center points of our souls. That kind of tie can be found between the women who stay and the children they keep—*in both adoptive and birthbound families.*

In the meantime, Rebecca and I have done the best of what we can do. For nearly fifteen years we have talked. We have summoned and relied on our instincts to coax our hurt and sins out of the corners. We have declared, to each other, our facts, fears, love, and regrets. For more than half her life, the force and persistence of our communication have both liberated and bound Rebecca and me. And that, finally, is why we are family.

Epilogue

Motherhood as Institution

The closer I have come to my essential motherhood, the more I am convinced that our cultural motherhood is an impossibility. We are flooded with images and edicts of correct maternity from our mothers, politicians, our children's fathers, from born-again Baptists, Freud, therapists, and even our own children. The loaded, indeed religious concept of motherhood is burdensome for the women expected to animate a culture's myth and for the girls expected to perpetuate it. The reliance and hopes pinned to our souls can be oppressive, leaving the most nurtured of children feeling fiercely unmothered, and the best-meaning mothers feeling empty and wrong.

As both a disappointed daughter and a besieged mother, I know the job description is destined always to eclipse and betray the work we actually do.

The heirs to the institution, our daughters, are among our mothers' most exacting critics. As daughters we scrutinize and blame, beg for protection, power, wisdom, and nurturance, with frenzied stage fright, knowing too well the performance our children will demand of us, because we have demanded it of our mothers. As reproducers of the species, we are cloying malcontents; we crowd one another with a panicky need to know: how to do it, how to be. Our daughters are our generational replacements, our tokens to immortality; we, their mothers, have the recipes.

And with each generation mothers want to make it better, encouraging their daughters to consider opportunities they didn't have or didn't dare realize. Yet while our mothers may gloat about our accomplishments, they are, at the same time, bitterly reminded that such plaudits were beyond their own reach. Modern daughters force mothers' uneasy self-reflection; they are us with more choices, our mothers are us with smaller plans. The messages from our mothers are mixed: Be like me, be yourself, learn my lessons, create your own. We want our girls to grow up, to see our lives beyond their experience, yet we guard our mother role with fire. Ambivalence between mothers and daughters, it seems, is almost inevitable.

My friend Merrill, who has a son, has said, "I'm glad I don't have a girl. I'm not proud of this, but I don't think I'm equal to the task. Raising a son is like waitressing; the work is hard but straightforward, and there's a tip on each table. Raising a girl seems so much more complex, demanding."

It's hard to say how much of Rebecca's and my struggle is common to most mothers and daughters. I do know we are denied the free play, the range of motion assumed by mothers and daughters who spar, hug, goof, sob, and scream within the assumed safety of mutual history. All the language and behavior between my birthdaughter and me is subject to a phantom translation, in our heads, by that awful spirit that presided over the day I walked away.

I know from mothering my kept children that the boundless strength of an unbroken tether is irreplaceable, and that, even under the best of circumstances, there is no substitute for it; there are only other ways. Sometimes I know I demand

and expect more of girls than I do of boys; whatever androgynous tendencies I see in my sons feel like triumphant milestones, crossovers out of the landscape of limited traditional male behavior into new, welcome ground. When they cook, talk, nurture, I beam with hope for the next generation of men and the women who may share their lives. My sons' self-reliance and comfort with emotions are historic, distinguishable achievements; but I expect as much from a daughter.

Abandoning fathers, though personae non gratae, are still woven seamlessly into our agenda of familial liabilities. When men leave their families, they are called, frivolously, deadbeats. A missing father's breach is financial. His emotional and psychological debts are not even implied. Recently birthfathers have begun to come forth, after the fact, staking a claim to the progeny who have been relinquished without their consent. While I admire the resolve of a genetic father to fight for his child, until fathers share the full responsibility of child rearing, such claims appear foolishly lopsided. They are presuming rights they have not yet gained.

For women, to renounce, dislike, or discontinue mothering is such a reprehensible infraction of our moral code that we primp to perfection the appearance of our maternity; we burnish the image to distraction and give ourselves over to indentured tenancy amid the Mother Marys to make the grade. If we've reneged, we hide in shame. We grow alienated from our own true instincts, our unique loving and real devotion—the choice of our kind of motherhood.

As a birthmother, I know the pity and jeers that are hurled at the women who walk away—the women who say "I quit," or simply "I can't," even when they give their children to someone who can—and are willing to suffer the loss. As one among the jeerers, embittered by my own mother's disappearance, and as a mother blamed by the daughter I left behind, I know that motherhood is saddled with many expectations but that the single most primal hunger a child has is for her mother to be there; being there is the necessary groundwork for growing, and our children know it.

But we cannot identify ourselves consistently and wholly in our adult lives by the way we were or were not mothered or fathered. If we are to go into adulthood, past our childlike demands for comfort, praise, and support, we must, at some reasonable age, demystify our parents and grow ourselves up. And then love our mortal mothers and their flawed, brave lives that much more.

Adoption

The business of women hatching babies for families who can't, the practice of a human being reduced to a womb for hire; of a baby becoming a supply for a demand, an export or coveted product, cannot, I believe, advance our culture's idea of women and children as people. In recent years, nontraditional adoptions—the selling of ova, the renting of uteri, and the contracting of reproductive abilities—have grown in popularity and been challenged regularly. Ultimately, the laws governing surrogate motherhood are made by and serve a privileged class of lawyers. The women who are most exploited by these laws usually have fewer resources and therefore less support, legal and otherwise, when they confront the awful reality of having to part with babies they carried and to whom they've grown attached. The women who benefit from laws allowing babies to be ordered, made, and delivered are the monied. The more specific the order—healthy, with preferential gender, age, and heritage—the higher the cost.

There are stories about certain actresses who have hired women physically similar to themselves, for many thousands of dollars, to be injected with their husbands' sperm and to bring babies to term for the express purpose of handing them over. This kind of deal emphasizes the objectification not only of the surrogate mother but of the custom-made baby; the lives of the natural mother and her baby are explicitly, perversely, secondary to the self-serving wishes of the financially capable. This kind of adoption is not about homeless babies; it is about shopping. Legally parenting a child is not a constitutional right, and there are too many babies waiting for homes to justify such a practice. Childless couples have far less right to a perfect child than a baby has a right to a parent, a home, and regular hugs. The adoptable, the motherless and fatherless, the ready and unloved—there are children waiting.

In the end, women must know that entering their bodies into business involves an unforgiving, low-return trade-off. And that the babies born of such deals will pay too.

Searching

Some will say that an adoptee's search for genetic relatives and the subsequent reunion of birthrelations bring on more questions than answers; that the awkward reconciliation causes anger, hurt, and doubts that are better left dormant, especially for the adoptive family.

My daughter would say: "What do people who adopt expect? They are bringing up another's child. This is a fact that can't be forgotten, lied about, or wished away. If your child has another family that's lost, it figures she may want to find it. When people ask me why I would want to know my birthfamily, I have to ask: Why wouldn't *anyone* want to know her mother, brothers, aunts, uncles?"

For Rebecca and many others, searching for authenticity (in the form of birth connections) means for once having control over an event that has felt, since memory, entirely out of their control. And often searching and finding is the better of two possible choices. The other is to wonder what could be known with work, *their* work.

The reason most often given by adoptees for wanting to search is a desire to know their medical histories, not necessarily because it is the real reason but because it is the least insulting and most acceptable. Many adoptees don't feel they have the right to need to know.

According to Kate Burke, president of the American Adoption Congress in Washington, DC, most of the hundreds of thousands of Americans looking for long-lost relatives are women searching for other women—birthmothers seeking the daughters they gave up years before, or, more typically, female adoptees in their late twenties or early thirties hoping to find their original mothers.

Male adoptees tend to search for their biological relatives less frequently. As sons, they seem to hold a pro forma loyalty to and protectiveness of their adoptive mothers, afraid they may feel betrayed if they, their sons, seek other mothers. Some men do not have the language to justify a search that may heal a wound they haven't the words to explain or have not felt permitted to suffer. Daughters, while they know the discomfort such a pursuit may cause, often trust their female relatives' ability to understand, or to have, at least, the training to talk it out. And for many women the search takes on a consuming urgency.

For some men, the birth process seems a distant event. For women, it is near and personal, and when female adoptees have babies it is often a profound and passionate milestone— they have made their first (biological) relatives—which stirs up grave questions about their own births and triggers a yen to hunt for answers. When some women have babies, they know the transcendental joy the birth of their children brings and often cannot understand how their own mothers could have walked away from, or never experienced, the euphoria they felt when delivering their own children. Only a defect, they reason, in the abandoned child could account for an act of such cold disassociation during a moment so blessed.

And for all adoptees there is a chance that another encounter with their original mothers may result in yet another rejection—an emotional setback not worth the risk.

But open adoption is not *the* answer, because in adoption there are no answers per se. Some proponents of open adoption presume that when the adoptive and birth families meet in an honest, accepting setting, the birthmother is able to resolve the guilt or grief of having given away her baby and the birthchild is able to learn her origins and erase her feelings of rejection. But this case can be deceptive, implying that the woman who is about to live or has already lived with loss for what is usually years will be cured by meeting the baby she lost and will never have as her child; and that the birthchild, having met the woman who gave her away, will no longer feel relinquished.

Sometimes, a reconnection with one's birthparent or parents can solidify existing family ties for the adoptee. Lisa, an adoptee and friend, has said, "My mother supported my search. She said, 'I can't be too involved, but tell me if I can help.'" When Lisa found a birthmother who was not prepared for the reappearance of a daughter or for any kind of lasting connection, it strengthened Lisa's bond with her (adoptive) mother. She said, "I knew then that my mother was my mother. The fantasy mother was not to be, so I had to find myself. I had to do the work of a grown-up. And my mother and I worked it out."

The day she met her birthmother, Lisa went to see her mother immediately after. "Mom, I'm home," she announced. Her mother told her she had stayed in that night because she was thinking of her, and a reconnection of another kind—unexpected and welcome—began.

"I wanted to find out [about my birthmother]," Lisa explained. "Doing the search let me know my [adoptive] mother in another way, and let me see how she loved me through it. She never said, 'How can you do this to me?' She knew I had to do it. I had been dealing with multiple realities, double mirrors, a birth certificate that was made up as if I didn't exist. Adoption is the biggest family secret. You need that information."

An ongoing reunion can create a format in which to work out the questions and offers a chance for a relationship to begin; but birthrelations are complicated families for which there is meager social precedent and recognition. It will always be a dangerous trial. As far as easing the grief, for the birthrelations, adoption is comparable to losing a limb, and, as every amputee knows, there will always be phantom pain.

Myths and Images

Over the last half of this century, the perception of adoptees has lurched from one extreme to another. The image of the surrendered child was once of a mysterious, good-hearted, but most likely from trash, ever-strange urchin-outsider (as in Edith Wharton's novel *Summer,* in which an adopted girl from the metaphorically dark mountain can never fit or find happiness in the plains below). Now, the adoptees we are reading or hearing about are children who are fought over, back-ordered, *created* even in order to fill cribs in childless homes.

The image of birthmother, however, has barely shifted, if her existence is acknowledged at all.

Living through the DeBoers-Schmidt fiasco in the summer

of 1993 (in which a birthmother fought for and won custody of her baby after two years of excessive media coverage and court battles) felt for me like being trapped in a fitful hallucination. What the press had to say and what the public sentiment seemed to be were so utterly opposite of what I was feeling and believed to be true that I was sure the story I was reading was not the story being read by most. The DeBoers were portrayed as loving parents stalked unjustifiably by a lying thief—the birthmother who couldn't seem to keep a man, her baby, or a promise.

What no one seemed to want to know is that Cara Clausen, Jessica's original mother, had asked for her baby back nine days after she relinquished her; that Clausen was acting on an impulse buried by most birthmothers when she requested the return of her child within days after giving her up; that the DeBoers had sought an unofficial adoption because they did not want to wait the customary three to six months until legal finalization of the surrender and because they wanted a white infant girl in perfect health; that the responsibility for the unnaturally long geographic distance between Baby Jessica and her natural parents lay with the DeBoers, who were willing to wage the ensuing court battle that would place their would-be adoptive daughter at the center of a disastrous cross fire, even though they were aware of the good chance that Jessica might have to shift families in the end. The DeBoers called in and worked the press like professionals, *creating* the trauma from which Jessica would have to recover.

Clausen's failure to reveal the father's identity immediately after the baby's birth is not uncommon among birthmothers whose shame and grief can inhibit their own confrontation with the facts of their ordeal. Often, the birthmother cleans up and hides the evidence (which includes the accomplice, the birthfather) as if she has committed a sickening offense. Clausen contacted Dan Schmidt, whom she later married, when she knew she could not endure the loss of her baby. Perhaps she believed that Schmidt, even though he was believed to have abandoned two other children before Jessica's birth, could be the protective soldier who would fight the battle with far more credibility than a woman who had reneged on motherhood once and briefly.

The unspoken sentiment in the DeBoer–Schmidt custody battle was that anyone's child is better off with a higher class of people. The DeBoers lived in a college town, and were lithe and soft-spoken. The Schmidts were working-class people. Dan was a truckdriver; he was loud, pissed off, and burly. Cara had had casual sex with a man she lied to. In the version of their story the DeBoers sold to television, Dan and Cara live in a trailer decorated with hubcaps. In a later interview, Dan Schmidt said he'd never lived in a trailer and thought the hubcaps looked silly.

In the months surrounding the Supreme Court's decision to return Jessica to her birthparents, there was a flood of articles blasting the legal system's bias against adoptive parents and the barriers to adoption in general. One columnist suggested that laws be changed so that no one who lies ("as Cara Schmidt did") could be permitted to benefit from that falsehood. (Having custody of her own child is a benefit?) Other journalists called Schmidt insensitive and selfish. She was indicted in the press for having lied, for telling the truth, for giving up her baby, and for wanting her back.

Other editorials pointed out that the DeBoers never officially adopted Jessica and could have returned her to the Schmidts when she was too young to experience "the full trauma of separation." (What about the trauma of separation from her original mother?) Yet, one editorial stated, the

DeBoers chose to fight on because "adoptive parents often bond with their child within weeks"; "so," the writer concluded, "the Schmidts' obstinacy is understandable." This writer, it seems, meant not to forgive the Schmidts' stubbornness, because their fight never seemed just, but that of the DeBoers, whose "honorable" battle aroused the sympathy of most. The results of polls were printed everywhere: "Seventy-eight percent in poll says adoptive parents should keep Jessica"; "Only 8 percent said she should be raised by her biological parents."

Another columnist argued that if it were not for a misguided faith in biology, foster children would not be waiting hopelessly for families. In fact, the lack of loving families willing to adopt these children (often older and nonwhite) is a key factor in keeping foster homes full. Other barriers are financial. When the cost of adoption can be between $20,000 and $30,000, otherwise qualified people who want to adopt will be screened out, leaving the children and the childless separated by class.

A year after the DeBoer–Schmidt trial, the media checked in on Anna Schmidt (the former Jessica DeBoer) and her family to report on her posttraumatic progress or lack thereof. A television piece featured a cheerful, affectionate child, a comfortable member of the Schmidt family. A weekly newsmagazine reported that although Anna became sad occasionally when Peach Street (her former address) was brought up, she had adjusted quite nicely to life with her biological parents and younger sister, Chloe.

But, even after the drawn-out, strenuous debate, there remains an unsettling degree of ignorance about adoption. In the magazine cover story, one expert offered a warning about the long-term effects of Anna's severance—from the DeBoers. Without a trace of irony, the professional advised:

"You really don't know what will happen with a crack in the foundation until it's asked to weather some external force." Anna's first and most profound "crack," separation from her biological mother at birth, is never mentioned. Psychologists need to be trained more thoroughly in their understanding of the experience of surrender and adoption.

The Cara Schmidts among us still arouse our contempt; the collective sentiment seems mired in a centuries-old, Hawthornesque idea of a soiled woman—indeed, a woman who has dared to humiliate the family order. Over the years adoptive parents have consistently been seen as the generous home providers they are. Taking in another's child will and should always be a natural act. But there is much to learn, and less to deny, when *real* stories are confronted.

The degree to which we play with and obscure the truth, whatever it may be, is a measure of the pain inherent in the experience. We dance around the reality of adoption as if we were dodging hot coals or thunderbolts, dedicated to constructing fables in order to tolerate the searing complexities.

I am waiting for adoption to be seen in daylight.

Rebecca and I have gone over a year without psychodramatic incident—a long time for us. She has accepted with generosity and courage my retirement from our cycles of rage and remorse. She has championed this book from the start, even though she knew that some of what I would write might hurt. We have arrived at what feels like a resting place—we have sampled relative tranquillity, where everything I say or do does not have the power to crush her, and everything she says or does will not be adjusted by me. My birthdaughter, in her middle twenties, is just beginning to unravel it all, on her own terms, and continues to search for answers she knows may forever elude her grasp.

While Rebecca was writing a book about black women writers, I sent her a postcard and wrote that I couldn't wait to read it because I knew it would be good. She answered:

Dear Jan,

. . . In an article I read about Maya Angelou right after the inaugural poem, she said that when she was about nineteen or twenty her mother told her that she had a rare combination of intelligence and kindness. And Maya said, "She's very intelligent, and she's too nice to lie. So, just suppose she is right? Suppose I really am somebody?" And she said it was the first time she ever remembered being on this earth as opposed to being part of it. I think I may have mentioned this to you before, but it struck me so deeply. We wait for these words from the women who gave us life. We just do. When you tell me that you know what I do will be good, it is important. Very. Thank you.

I sent a postcard saying that she was right, that our mothers' praise is their implicit joy in our existence. "And," I wrote, "I am glad you exist. Very."

In the last year Rebecca has grown in unimaginable ways. She has never been so recognizable. When she turned twenty-five, she turned a corner. But that is another story. Hers.

Rebecca's parents and I have not spoken for years. It is not what I have wanted, but the weight of Rebecca's and my journey, so constant and tense, must have taken its toll. With me, in all our encounters, Linette has shown only the most profound generosity. She has given Rebecca the chance to know her other mother, a gift I know springs from her abiding love for her daughter—a gift that I cannot even begin to imagine giving.

Long after her death, regrettably, it has become clear to me that the biological stranger in our midst, my grandmother Altie H. Smith, unwittingly confronted head-on the mulish demons of adoption. When gathering my family stories, I kept remembering the strength of the lessons I had learned from her. I found myself drawn, against my expectations, to her large, durable image and unique courage. I will never forget her consistently willful acceptance of the members of her family, her principled advocacy of us, and her unyielding presence in the face of birth, death, sorrow. She fought for us with intrepid loyalty; she stayed with us through it all.

Restless days will revisit Rebecca and me, forever perhaps. But the stories I found by going back and looking hard have brought the peace of resolve, away from, for once, the oppressive harangue of doubt and everyone else's meaning of *mother*. I have founded an adulthood "based on a party of one," as my mother would say, fortified by a defiant self-reliance, damned not to repeat dead-end errors.

It has taken many years of learning and daring to let others in, to get close; more than anyone else my sons have taught me how. While they occasionally refer to me as their "choremaster" (they became acquainted early on, as I did, with the rigors of household maintenance), I have over the years been happy to prepare their neatly packaged lunches. Their unwavering presumption of my place in their lives confirms the faith in me I've wanted them to have. Their easy love is my home.

When I first heard the voice of my birthgrandmother, Mavis Peabody, it was on the phone and she was irritated. (Who was I to call—how did I get her number?—and say that she had had a daughter by that name?) Since then we have straightened out names, and Mavis, who has no kept children of her own, has been gracious about filling in the details of a previously blurred family history.

For most of the last twenty-five years, until she moved to Maryland, Mavis has lived within twenty minutes of me, within an hour of her daughter, and we, grandmother and granddaughter, have at different times shared the same employer and lived on the same street. Three blood-fused generations, like truant satellites, have orbited the same communities within feet of one another at times, and never known.

My biological grandmother parted with two children before and one child after she gave my mother to the Smiths, under a variety of desperate circumstances. When Mavis got pregnant for the third time, with my mother, she was living at home. Mavis's mother, Clara, could take no more, called the town clerk, had her daughter declared a pauper, and announced she no longer had a child named Mavis. After Mavis and her infant daughter were released from the hospital, they took up residence at the local poorhouse. Mavis left town fourteen months later, after she had met a man with whom she wanted to travel. She decided to give her daughter to the Smiths.

Mavis said her mother was bothered in the extreme by everything she did, and until recently, in her eighties, she did not understand why. Now, she says, it makes sense. When she was fourteen, Clara Jones, Mavis's mother, was disowned by her mother, Sylvia Spears. Sylvia had wanted to jettison her four children, so she could be free to be with a man with whom she had fallen in love (her husband had died the previous year). Two brothers were sent to live with the Shaker community, the younger daughter went with her mother, and Clara was on her own. She never forgave, spoke to, or saw her mother again. No wonder my mother was hard on me, Mavis said, sorting out her revelation. I was doing what her mother had done.

Over the past year, Mavis has mentioned more than once that knowing my brother and me is a treasure she thought she would never have. She, too, is a prolific and able letter writer, and, like her birthdaughter, she is a believer in fair treatment for all—a true egalitarian.

As I started to leave her Maryland apartment one late afternoon, Mavis came close and said she did not know how she would feel if she were to meet the daughter she gave away. "It's been a long time," she said apologetically, looking away. "I don't think I would have, you know, feelings for her." God, I said, I understood. I have told her that my mother, her birthdaughter, does not want to meet her and that she is somewhat reclusive. Mavis has said that, as far as she knows, there is no mental illness in her family. My mother's biological father is a mystery.

Only occasionally do we discuss the subject of adoption. But in December 1992, Mavis wrote to me about what must have been on her mind for years:

Dear Jan:

You mentioned in one of your letters that your mother said she had always felt like an orphan and had no birth affiliations. And I thought about that. I could certainly understand why she would feel that way.

At the time of her birth, I was very ill with what in those days was called childbed fever (septicemia) . . . under the circumstances I could not nurse the baby, or even see her. I . . . saw the baby but once, when a girl brought her out from the nursery and held her at the foot of the bed. When we were taken to the poorhouse we were given a room next to the Nurses' Station. . . . Of course the nurses . . . were delighted with her—all their patients were old and sick or mental patients waiting to go to Danvers—and suddenly here was a beautiful, good-natured, happy baby.

So as you can see, Ruth Ann had many mothers during the first year of her life—and there was no way she could have known which one of us was her real mother.

They talk a lot these days about "bonding"—as you can see by the above Ruth Ann and I never had a chance to bond—and so I certainly understand how she feels. I am sorry, of course, that it happened, but I did the best I could but eventually felt that it wasn't fair to her and that she deserved a mother and father and a stable home life. I hope you all understand that I thought I was doing what was best for her.

Yours—
Mavis

After nearly a year of knowing my biological grandmother, I struggle with my indifference to her, though I am always struck by how kind she is in her letters. I will never understand how she could have given away all four of her children. Nothing she says seems to deliver the reasons I need to understand the debt my mother has paid because of an early abandonment by her original mother (the same sad frustration Rebecca must feel when I fail to deliver the cure). Sometimes when Mavis tells her tales, all I hear is her oblivion to the hurt she has planted.

What means everything to me—children, relinquished and kept, and my responsibility for them and to myself—has slipped her mind. This woman, my mother's mother, though I know she has barriers and baggage made of pain, often feels like a stranger to me. It is perhaps unfair for me to have expected more.

The last time I saw my mother, in early 1994, was the day

my brother and I took her to the home of her birthmother. After a year of knowing she could, my mother finally decided to travel to Maryland to meet her. The afternoon reunion in Mavis's apartment was uneventful. My mother was polite and somewhat interested. Mavis told her stories, of which she was the featured player, without a hint of visible concern for the daughter she had abandoned who now sat in a chair across from her, listening quietly.

When my mother asked plaintively, "Who was my father?" Mavis responded with, "What kind of a question is that?!" as if her birthdaughter had posed a most unreasonable riddle. She scowled. And paused. My mother, she finally explained, was the product of "what you'd now call date rape."

"I was hoping you wanted to because you liked him," my mother said, smiling over the awkwardness of learning, rather bluntly, that her father was a rapist and that her very existence was the result of a bad night in her mother's history.

"No, not at all," Mavis answered with disgust, clearly more interested in boasting and being excused than in her relinquished daughter's vulnerable question.

After we returned home, we visited my mother's biological aunt, Mavis's sister Grace, who is endearingly blunt. After introductions, Grace began talking about her sister.

"You know," Grace said, "I once asked Mavis, 'Did you *ever* think how your actions may have affected your family, or other people besides yourself?' And you know what she said? 'No.' Just like that. No, she said, she hadn't thought about it at all."

My mother laughed. "That's kind of refreshing. I like that."

Grace twisted her eighty-seven-year-old neck out to fasten

her gaze on this new relative and asked incredulously, "You find *that* admirable?"

Yes, my mother answered defiantly, she did.

And I believed her, despite the terrible irony of it.

Earlier in the day, Mavis had talked about a most unusual case of "amnesia" that had afflicted her regarding all things prior to 1936, the year she gave away her last and fourth child. Over the years my mother had invoked the "System" that had invaded her life and had caused her to stop being our mother when my brother and I were eleven and twelve. My mother and Mavis had claimed an otherworldly absence during the years they had committed the abandoning. Both Mavis and her genetic daughter had created technical interferences to explain the maternal resignations for which they could not and would never be responsible.

Later that day my brother called.

"What do you think?" he asked.

"About the reunion? In my opinion it was hugely ex post facto. Unepiphanous. Lives have been lived. Sara's sixty. Mavis is eighty-five. Who cares?"

My brother agreed and added that for our mother, the reunion was probably marginally better than living with the regret of not having met her mother, when she knew she had the choice.

"Yeah, and if she takes anything away from this, maybe it will be a renewed sense of who her *real* mother was. I hope."

Two days later I received a letter from my mother.

"Mavis has nice legs," my mother wrote, "like mine, but other than that—"

A f t e r w o r d
b y   R e b e c c a

It is truly heartening to join Jan here in this Afterword, in company with her words, her strength and compassion, our journey together, and the still and many unanswered questions.

When an adoption takes place, adoptees are usually not able to speak, let alone express our complex feelings about how we will feel in, say, ten years, when we do a family tree in school and don't have the information, or in twenty-five years, when we think about having children of our own. Sometimes my dread outweighs the joy at the prospect of giving birth, because I am afraid an experience so epiphanous will spur the striking realization of my own (birth)mother going through the same experience with me and then giving me up and it will break me. And if it doesn't destroy me, I will never be able to be a good enough mother, because I was never a good enough daughter, not good enough to keep anyway.

I often find myself trying to forget that I was adopted, because if I hadn't been adopted, the love I feel for Jan would be simple and the ever-present feeling of betrayal I have toward my parents would not exist. For people who choose adoption, there must be an overriding awareness that, after all is said and done, all the happy endings in the world cannot change the *facts:* the fact of a woman giving away her child; the fact of a child feeling abandoned; the fact that people are parenting a child who is not theirs. There will never be an adoptive experience that does not require emotional courage, and what may often seem like impossible communication skills. And it is work.

It was my adoptive parents' belief that a child's first breath reveals a unique will and that will should be nurtured and encouraged, not shaped into something other than what it is. I believe my parents mistook my feelings of abandonment, vis-à-vis my need for attention, and nurtured me to a point where I literally expected everyone to respond to me in the same way. When I met Jan, I waited impatiently for her to follow suit, along with everyone else in my eleven-year-old life who considered me a rare, dark jewel from faraway lands. But she didn't. Not only did Jan know something about abandonment and its repercussions from her own childhood and lost relationship with her mother, but her style of parenting is very different from that of my parents. Jan would say that kids need guidelines to build their own values alongside or against. If a child is left to be whoever and whatever she wants, how will she know who or what to be? And for an adoptee, being raised with such freedom is profoundly unsettling.

After I met Jan on that summer day in 1980, all I wanted was her love and some kind of guarantee that she would never leave me again. Before we met, I had some information about Jan, but mostly I had fantasies. By the time we met she had become, in my mind, immortal. The resentment and anger I had about her abandoning me didn't come until long after we met, when I discovered that she was actually human. It was easier to forgive her when I thought of her as unearthly, because no human on this earth would ever give away her child.

The first few years of knowing each other were tough. I hated her. First for refusing to claim the immortal status I had given her, and second for not loving me instantly and unconditionally, which is how I had been taught to receive love. It's one of those phases that leaves a creepy, gooey feeling at the base of your neck. I didn't think for a minute that she, at twenty-eight with two new babies, wouldn't know how to deal with *me*. She had had me before those two new babies, thank you very much, and I felt like her giving me up was a huge mistake and now she had the chance to make up for it. You laid down to make me, I thought, now stand up and raise me. Today, as I struggle with a residual self-importance and my feelings of entitlement, I am grateful to her for not doing what I thought she should have done. I realize that she was the only one who was saying, "Whoa, wait a minute here."

Now, almost fifteen years after reuniting, Jan and I trust each other. Our love is finally kind. And the reasons for this are clear. We have created, through love and our struggle, a language for our relationship that was and continues to be desperately needed. Without language, there is no communication, and what cannot be communicated cannot exist.

About the Author

JAN WALDRON lives in New England with her family.